The 50 Greatest Pirates

EVERY FAN SHOULD KNOW

Lew Freedman

Blue River Press
Indianapolis

www.brpressbooks.com

The 50 Greatest Pittsburgh Pirates Every Fan Should Know

Published by Blue River Press
Indianapolis, Indiana
www.brpressbooks.com

Distributed by Cardinal Publishers Group
2402 N. Shadeland Avenue, Suite A
Indianapolis, IN 46219
317-352-8200 phone
317-352-8202 fax
www.cardinalpub.com

ISBN: 9781935628330

Cover Design by Phil Velikan
Cover Photos of Honus Wagner Courtesy of the
National Baseball Hall of Fame Library
Book design by Dave Reed

Printed in the United States of America

10 9 8 7 6 5 4 3 2 1

Contents

INTRODUCTION

Having the nickname Pirates has always meant that the Pittsburgh baseball team had a sort of cool, swashbuckling look to it, even when nobody talked about baseball teams being cool.

Although the Pirates lost much of their dazzling allure between 1992 and 2012 when they recorded 20 straight losing seasons, the most among the four major sports in American history, the mojo seems to be back in Pittsburgh with the qualification of the 2013 team for the National League playoffs and scoring 90-plus victories.

From despair to giddiness, Pirates fans are back on the bandwagon. As one of the traditional franchises in baseball, that's the way it should be, and a whole new generation of heroes, led by Andrew McCutchen, is making nice with the Pittsburgh sports fan that was hungry for a winner.

The Pirates date their history uninterruptedly to 1882 when they were the Pittsburgh Alleghenys. The Alleghenys were first organized in 1876, but didn't hold together and then joined the International League six years later. While there have been gaps when pennants were rare commodities, the team has given the baseball world many prominent players worth cheering, and several notable, memorable teams, ever since.

They even have a former owner, in Barney Dreyfuss, in the Baseball Hall of Fame. Dreyfuss helped create the World Series and spearheaded construction of Forbes Field.

The Pirates played in the first World Series, losing to the Boston Red Sox. Dreyfuss bought the Pirates in 1900 and in order to stock the team he acquired 14 players from the defunct Louisville Colonels. One of those was Hall of Famer Honus Wagner.

Pittsburgh won its first pennant in 1901 and followed up with National League championships in 1902 and 1903. The first World Series was conducted in 1903, with the NL winner facing the fledgling American League's winner. Dreyfuss lobbied for the invention of the showdown to select a true champion.

The club won its first World Series in 1909 and won again in 1925. The Pirates won the NL pennant in 1927, but lost to the New York Yankees in that Series. That New York team was the Babe Ruth-led bunch known as "Murderers Row," which some consider the finest single-season club of all time.

Some pennant drought years followed and there were some truly horrendous seasons in the early 1950s. When things were at their bleakest slugger Ralph Kiner arrived on the scene to provide some excitement. Kiner, a genial man, led the National League in home runs seven years in a row in the late 1940s and early '50s.

However, the Pirates captured America's heart in 1960 when they won the title as underdogs against the New York Yankees. Bill Mazeroski's walk-off home run in the ninth inning of the seventh game might be the most important single hit in baseball history.

In 1971 the Pirates again fielded an appealing team that operated under the leadership of Willie "Pops" Stargell, which won another Series. Stargell was a player that young teammates listened to and who could energize a ball park with his home-run power.

A common theme between the 1960 club and the 1971 team was that Danny Murtaugh, the most beloved manager in team history, ran both squads.

In 1971, with no fanfare, Murtaugh became the first manager to field a team of all blacks. He didn't make a big deal out of it—and neither did the players since some didn't even realize it until the game ended. But that was a milestone in a sport that was only a quarter century removed from banning participation of all African-Americans.

Manager Chuck Tanner led the Pirates to another world championship in 1979 with the "We Are Family" song by Sister Sledge borrowed as a theme song.

Along the way the Pirates have been blessed with many great players. Jake Beckley was the best player in the pre-1900 era. Wagner won eight National League batting titles and is usually picked as the shortstop on all-time teams. There is a statue of Wagner outside of the current Pirates home, PNC Park. Speedster Max Carey was a big contributor at the same time.

They were followed by brothers Paul and Lloyd Waner, both terrific hitters, who were called "Big Poison" and "Little Poison" and Harold "Pie" Traynor, one of the finest third basemen of all time.

Elroy Face was one of the sport's great early relievers, able to shut down late-inning threats with his forkball.

Unlike some franchises where there is an undisputed No. 1 player in team history, while the nod goes to Wagner, there are definitely some true believers in Roberto Clemente. Clemente was not only a Hall of Fame player, but a Hall of Fame person who died in the act of a mission undertaken to help save lives. Clemente is also the player most admired by Latino players from all teams as a symbol of one of the first Hispanics to make it big in the region's favorite sport.

Over the years the Pirates played home games at Exposition Park, Forbes Field, which opened in 1909 as one of the first two steel and concrete stadiums constructed to replace flimsy wooden parks, then the less-favored Three Rivers Stadium, and finally PNC Park, right downtown. Three Rivers Stadium was an aptly named park in a city built on a point of land where the Allegheny, the Monongahela and the Ohio Rivers come together. But it was one of the unhappy cookie-cutter-type stadiums that opened in the early 1970s. The round-shaped stadium, which also played host to the Pittsburgh Steelers, was drably interchangeable with stadiums in Philadelphia and St. Louis.

Some of the greatest Pirates pitchers were in the rotation long, long ago. Wilbur Cooper (202), Babe Adams (194), Sam Leaver (193), and Deacon Phillippe (167) were several of the biggest winners in Pittsburgh history, but retired decades ago. Vern Law, winner of the 1960 Cy Young Award, will always have a special place in the hearts of Pittsburgh fans for his 20-win season during that World Series championship year.

Although he only spent a portion of his career with the Pirates, Vic Willis did magical things with a baseball before 1910, his earned run average while representing Pittsburgh registering 2.09.

The task of choosing the top 50 players in Pirates history was a challenging one. Although the debate between Wagner and Clemente for No. 1 was not a riddle that could be avoided, most of the top ten was self-explanatory. The real battle always comes in determining if someone makes the list at all or can't pass the cut because the competition is too stiff.

Some very popular Pirates players are not among the top 50. Not because they weren't good players, but because there were other players who arguably did more for the team during their stay.

Some players from so long ago that none of us still living remember anything about them have superb statistics and were intrinsic members of the Pirates a few generations ago. Some players we grew up with, were favorites, but don't have a strong enough record for inclusion. Occasionally a player remembered for significant contributions turns out not to have made even one All-Star team.

The top 50 list is bound to cause debate. Not everyone will be satisfied with it. Some people are bound to say, "How could you leave so-and-so off?"But 50 means 50, even if 70 guys are deserving. That is partially attributable to the fact that the Pirates have been around a long time.

Harvey Haddix was left off. He never won more than 12 games in a season for the Pirates and pitched for other teams. However, he did pitch baseball's greatest game ever thrown for Pittsburgh when he hurled 12 perfect innings against the Milwaukee Braves in 1959, only to lose 1-0 in the 13th.

The founding year of 1882 was 132 years ago. A lot of Pirate baseball has been played and many, many top-notch players have worn the team colors and pledged allegiance to the Bucs symbol with the eye patch.

Up until 1924, only seven times was the Pirates leading home-run hitter for a season able to reach double figures and no one smashed more than 13 in a year. Those seasons were played during the deadball era.

Not surprisingly, none of those players from way back make into the team's top 10 for homers. But in an era when starting pitchers finished their games and relief pitching was pretty much considered a dirty phrase, some amazing single-season pitching marks were recorded.

In 1887, Pud Galvin threw 440 2/3 innings. Pretty amazing, huh? But that's not the Pirates'/Alleghenys' single-season record. In 1888, a fellow by the name of Ed Morris threw 480 innings. There were no follow-up reports available indicating that his arm fell off, but it might have.

The sport was still baseball in the 1880s, 1920s, 1950s, 1980s, just as it is in the 2000s. Rules change, techniques change, but the players all played for the same organization.

— Lew Freedman
September, 2013

Courtesy of the National Baseball Hall of Fame Library

Honus Wagner is considered one of the true icons of baseball, winner of eight batting titles and honored with a statue outside the Pirates' PNC Park. Some believe the shortstop was the best player of all.

1
HONUS WAGNER

Known as "The Flying Dutchman," Honus Wagner is not only one of the greatest baseball players of all time, one of his baseball cards is the most valuable of all time. In Pittsburgh, the card is secondary to the man. Wagner won eight National League batting titles (later equaled by Tony Gwynn), and he remained with the franchise for decades as a coach after retirement.

In that way, future generations of Pirates fans who never got the chance to see Wagner patrol at shortstop, or wield one of the most dangerous bats in the history of the sport, got to see him up close in a Pittsburgh uniform anyway.

Although many fans think of Wagner as a Pittsburgh-only player, he actually broke into the majors with Louisville in 1897 and became a Pirate for the rest of his career in 1900 – a season in which he hit a career-high .381 and won his first batting crown. Despite playing on three Pirates pennant-winners, and competing in the first World Series in 1903, Wagner said winning that first batting crown by one point over Elmer Flick, was his biggest thrill in the game.

Wagner was born in 1874 in Chartiers, Pennsylvania. His father was a coal miner and he had eight siblings, though three died at a very young age. Wagner played 21 years in the big leagues and hit .328. He was such a renowned fielder, hitter, and gentleman that Pittsburgh erected a statue to honor him and the likeness has moved from ballpark to ballpark as the Pirates have.

The 5-foot-11, 200-pound Wagner stopped taking his cuts for the Pirates in 1917, meaning he played his entire career in the deadball era. Wagner played in 2,794 games, collected 3,420 hits, drove in

1,733 runs, stole 723 bases, twice led the National League in hits, three times led in triples, and seven times led the NL in doubles.

Wagner clouted 101 home runs without facing lively ball pitching and some years later marveled at what he might have accomplished if he played a little bit later.

"If I were 20 years younger, the way baseballs are thrown today," Wagner said when he was 55, "I would hit .450."

One way that Wagner's fame has been perpetuated is the rare baseball card he is pictured on that was issued as a 1910 T-206 tobacco card. The story has always gone that the card is so hard to obtain, and its value has grown insanely, because only a small number are in the marketplace, and that stems from Wagner asking the company to stop selling them. Many years later, Wagner's grand-daughter told a sportswriter that his objection was that children had to buy tobacco to get the card, not that he was against tobacco use per se since he chewed it. Over the years a few dozen of the cards have surfaced, but in prime condition it has sold for nearly three million dollars.

Wagner neither reaped a bounty from the card, nor lived long enough to see it reach an astronomical value in the card collecting hobby. He died at 81 in 1955.

He fell on hard times as a businessman after breaking into baseball at a salary of $35 a month, and that was one reason he stuck around the Pirates as a coach for years. Wagner knew his stuff when it came to hitting. He studied the pitchers of his day.

"I used to know the foot movement and arm movement of every pitcher in the league," Wagner said.

New York Giants long-time manager John J. McGraw always said the best ball player he saw was Wagner. Ed Barrow, the Hall of Fame executive of the Red Sox and Yankees, and Fred Clarke, a Hall of Fame Wagner teammate, all believed that Wagner was the best player of all.

And Christy Mathewson, McGraw's ace, who won 373 games, said it was never a treat facing Wagner from the mound.

"Hans Wagner has always been a hard man for me," Mathewson said, "but in that I have nothing on a lot of other pitchers. He takes a long bat, stands well back from the plate and steps into the ball. He is what is known as a free swinger."

Mathewson said that when he was a young pitcher and still learning his way around the National League he asked his catcher, Jack Warner, what Wagner's weakness was. Warner answered without a smile, saying, "A base on balls." In other words, the only safe play with Wagner was to walk him.

Compared to the physiques of hard-body modern players who lift weights, Wagner did not look imposing. He was bow-legged, belying his swiftness on the base paths, was powerful through the chest, had long arms and large hands. He hit to all fields and batted over .300 16 times. Wagner won the NL batting title four years in a row between 1906 and 1909. Wagner never made more than $10,000 a year as a player.

It wasn't as if he was made to feel welcome in baseball at first, either. By the 1950s, when Wagner was fading, Major League baseball seemed like a brotherhood to him. The players on opposing teams fraternized and even knew one other from the minors, or as teammates through trades.

When Wagner broke in it was tough even for a rookie to get his batting practice swings in, never mind being friendly with a foe.

"I played half a season before I got up enough courage to speak to an opponent," Wagner said. "I was in right field one day and after the other club's right fielder hit two successive home runs, I remarked as we exchanged positions, "Nice hitting." He gave me a dirty look and in a sneering tone said, "Go to hell."

Wagner was mild-mannered when he showed up on the diamond, but even his own teammates were rude to the youngster, so he had to stand his ground or fight back. He once took a cut at a ball that came within an inch of smashing in the jaw a teammate who had spit tobacco juice on Wagner's shoes. He had to be that way—tougher—or be run off.

After putting his superb seasons in, Wagner was greeted more cordially by most. He had gained a bit of respect and in some quarters was called, "Mr. Baseball."

As he watched the new lively ball era dawn, Wagner did not pine for the old days, nor stick with the theme that the players of his era were all better than the younger generations. He watched with amazement as Babe Ruth and other sluggers came along. That prompted him to write a magazine story in 1940 pleading with help for the battered pitchers, his enemies of yore.

"Help the poor pitcher!" Wagner said. "Give him a break, or the second hundred years of baseball are going to be the hardest. Baseball is going to become a game destitute of pitchers unless something is done to restore the balance between hitting and pitching."

That was funny stuff coming from a player who beat up on pitchers regularly for more than two decades, even if it wasn't always by peppering homers. Wagner abused them every other which way.

There were always tests, always ways in which a player had to measure up to show that he belonged in the show. Ty Cobb was a great one for taking things out on rookies to see if they had the right stuff. The Pirates played Cobb's Detroit Tigers in the 1909 World Series and Cobb got on base. He yelled to Wagner that he was going to steal second on the next pitch, announcing his intention with bravado, as well as insult, calling Wagner "Krauthead."

Sure enough, the ball was flung, Cobb high-tailed it to second, and there was Wagner, ball in hand, waiting to apply the tag. It was no gentle touch, either. Wagner rammed the ball into Cobb's mouth and not only shut him up, but made him obtain three stitches to stop the bleeding. That's one way to win respect.

Wagner's popularity never waned a bit in Pittsburgh. Not only did his achievements continue to glow, there he was in the flesh for years, still helping those Pirate batters. Wagner couldn't walk down the street without being stopped by fans, and his fan mail continued to mount up, even 30 years into retirement – and that was well before any baseball nostalgia or memorabilia craze took off.

Pittsburgh decided to erect its monument to him in the form of a statue, just in time for him to appreciate it. The Wagner statue was molded and unveiled in 1955, not long before Wagner passed away. He was not strong enough to participate in a ceremony, but viewed it from a parked car.

"No other player has ever brought more honor to the game of baseball than Honus Wagner," said former Pirates owner William Benswanger on that occasion.

Courtesy of the National Baseball Hall of Fame Library

Roberto Clemente was not only a hero in Pittsburgh, but to all Latin American players. A Hall of Fame outfielder with a phenomenal arm, he stroked 3,000 hits and won four batting titles before perishing on a mission of mercy to help earthquake victims in Nicaragua.

2
ROBERTO CLEMENTE

To Latin American players who followed him into the big leagues Roberto Clemente was an icon, a role model, a pioneer who helped pave the way for future generations of Spanish speaking players from Puerto Rico, the Dominican Republic and elsewhere. He was also a hero to Pittsburgh Pirates fans and the city of Pittsburgh for the manner in which he handled himself on and off the field.

For a time misunderstood, Clemente, in the end, transcended sport with the humanitarian efforts that cost him his life at 38.

Clemente the player was a proud athlete of tremendous physical skills, who could run, hit, throw and field. He was 5-foot-11 and his playing weight was listed as only 175 pounds, but he never seemed like a small player. He protected right field in spacious Forbes Field and in Three Rivers Stadium and his cannon arm scared the speed right out of opponents' feet. At the same time he batted .317 during his Major League career, all spent with the Pirates, and collected 3,000 hits exactly, reaching the milestone in his last game when no one realized it would be his last game.

Originally drafted by the Brooklyn Dodgers, Clemente was snagged by the Pirates when the Dodgers tried to stash him in the minors and not expose his talents. They failed. The Dodgers had given Clemente a $10,000 bonus and under the rules in effect at the time they had to keep him on the Major League roster for two years or risk losing him. They sent Clemente to Montreal, tried not to play him so much that he would be noticed, but they lost the risk. Pittsburgh, then under the administration of Branch Rickey, reaped the benefits.

The lithe, yet muscular outfielder broke into the majors in 1955 and played his final game at the end of the 1972 season. A few months later, on New Year's Eve, he perished in a plane crash as he accompanied a load of medical and foodstuffs to survivors of the Nicaraguan earthquake. The plane crashed on takeoff and Clemente's body was never found.

Clemente came to prominence at a time in American history when black athletes were just making their presence felt in baseball and when the country was still somewhat in the dark ages on race relations. In addition, his first language was Spanish and in contrast to the modern era when roughly 28 percent of Major League players are of Hispanic origin the idea of Spanish speakers representing a team like the Pirates was still somewhat of a rarity.

For some years Clemente rebelled against the simple, casual use by journalists who shortened Roberto to Bob. He felt discriminated against on two counts, his skin color and his Latino heritage, yet over time became a beloved Pittsburgh athlete whose contributions to the sport and to his fellow man live on long after his death.

"I feel I would be considered to be a much better athlete if I were not a black Latin," Clemente said once. "I play as good as anybody. But I am not loved. I don't need to be loved. I just wish that would happen."

Clemente sought the respect he felt he deserved from his accomplishments on the diamond, and they were substantial. Clemente played in more games with the Pirates than anyone else—2,433. He had that .317 lifetime average, won four batting titles and led the National League in hits twice. He was selected to 15 All-Star teams (including three times when there were two games in the same season) and won 12 Gold Gloves. And he was named the 1966 NL Most Valuable Player. Perhaps some of the recognition was later in coming than Clemente would have liked, but in the long run it did come.

For some time Clemente, who had a series of ailments, would try to make it clear that he was not lazy, but hurt, and what he said was often misconstrued. He was speaking English, but thinking in Spanish, and there often seemed to be a barrier between him and white sportswriters.

"This was the most decent man I've ever known," said former Pirate pitcher and long-time broadcaster Steve Blass. "And nobody seemed to ever understand him. Maybe there was a language barrier. I don't know. He was absolutely selfless."

As much as he loved baseball, Clemente always focused on the big picture and big issues. At one point during his career, even after he had been established as a star, he said he could never sleep. The stress did not come from baseball, but probably because he always had so much on his mind.

"I don't get tired from baseball," he said. "I'm tired because I can't sleep." He saw doctors and took sleeping pills, but could not find the magic formula. "None of them help. I went to a diagnostic clinic in Pittsburgh and spent four days getting examined. They said I was too tense, that I worried too much and that I couldn't find relaxation."

He pretty much always looked relaxed on the field, though, whether it was awaiting a fly ball in right field, or waiting for his pitch in the batter's box.

Clemente was a member of the revered 1960 Pirates World Series champs, the team that took out the New York Yankees in dramatic fashion in the seventh game. He was 25 at the time and he batted .310. In 1971 the Pirates were really his team. He was 36 and that year hit .414 in the Series and was named MVP.

For those willing to pay attention Clemente was most motivated by pride. He wanted to lead the league in categories to show that he was the best. All-Star selections and awards bestowed upon him were validation of his skills and so was a higher salary.

In 1967 Clemente was given a contract for $100,000 that made him the highest paid player in team history. To him it was his due, to others it was a milestone. In the modern baseball world Clemente would be making $20 million a year.

When he got a public forum, Clemente used it to make a variety of points. He often spoke up for Latino players whom he felt were overlooked and said the fact that they spoke Spanish was not an excuse for their achievements to go unrecognized or unrewarded. One thing he emphasized was that Latino players seemed to be overlooked for off-season invitations on the banquet circuit, which was a big thing over the winter in that era.

"Somebody told me it was too expensive to send for the Latins," Clemente said. "Do you know the round-trip air fare from Puerto Rico to New York is only $90? Somebody else said the Latins were hard to understand when they speak. Maybe we don't speak good English, but people know what we say. If you want somebody who speaks five languages, get somebody from the United Nations."

When Clemente won his MVP award, the sportswriters found him at home in Puerto Rico by telephone.

"I'm very happy," he said. "Very happy. This is a great honor. The only thing I would trade this for is a pennant."

The end of Clemente's career and the end of his life, are both the stuff of legend and lore.

As a player Clemente was closing in on the milestone of 3,000 hits, a figure that has made it pretty automatic for players to be enshrined in the Hall of Fame.

Clemente suffered through a difficult year in 1972, his last season. He did bat .312, but incurred several injuries that held him to participation in 102 games. On the last day of the regular season, the last at-bat of his career except for that season's post-season playoffs, Clemente smacked a double off the New York Mets' Jon Matlack for his 3,000th hit. Since Clemente had no intention of retiring most people just thought it was nice that he didn't have to wait through an entire off-season until the next year to obtain it.

Near the very end of the year, a large earthquake struck Managua, Nicaragua, spreading destruction and hardship. Clemente began fund-raising to aid survivors in need and with the $150,000 he received in donations he bought food and medical supplies for those stricken. He personally wished to accompany the plane on the mission to distribute the needed goods. And for that he paid with his life.

Clemente heard that supplies sent to Nicaragua had been intercepted by the greedy, so he wanted to make sure this fourth shipment was delivered into the right hands. The plane was overloaded by several thousand pounds and crashed off of Isla Verde in Puerto Rico.

The Baseball Hall of Fame waved its five-year waiting period and Clemente was elected almost immediately. The Pirates erected a statue in his honor and it stands outside PNC Park, their home today, the symbol of a vibrant hero overlooking the only team he represented in the majors.

Courtesy of the National Baseball Hall of Fame Library

Paul Waner, the older of the Waner brothers, was called "Big Poison." A remarkable hitter, he slashed 3,152 hits, batted .333 lifetime and won four National League batting titles.

3
PAUL WANER

Paul Waner was the older half of the most accomplished baseball brother duo in history. Along with his brother Lloyd the twosome came out of Oklahoma and spent years ripping big hits for the Pittsburgh Pirates.

The slightly higher achieving Paul played 20 years in the big leagues, mostly with the Pirates, finishing with a .333 average. He was the Most Valuable Player in the National League in 1927 when Pittsburgh won the pennant and advanced to the World Series and was a member of the 1925 championship team.

Although his career began several years before the All-Star game came into existence, Waner was selected for four All-Star appearances. He also won three batting titles. In 1927 Waner hit a career-high .380. In 1934 he won with a mark of .362. And in 1936 he won again with a .373 average.

Among his other top statistics, Waner collected 3,152 hits and among those were 605 doubles. He amassed 1,309 RBIs. In what might be the best pairing of nicknames, the Waner brothers were called "Big Poison" and "Little Poison."

Born in Harrah, Oklahoma in 1903, Paul Waner made his Major League debut in 1926. From the first moment that Waner stepped into a batter's box in the bigs he could hit. As a rookie he batted. 336, the first of 14 times he topped the .300 mark.

In his second season wearing a Pirate uniform Waner stroked 237 hits. Eight times he totaled at least 200 hits in a year.

Another Hall of Famer, whose career overlapped with Waner's was Heinie Manush and Manush thought the world of Waner.

"Pound for pound, Paul was the greatest," Manush said.

The reason Manush may have mentioned the poundage was that Waner was not a big guy. He stood 5-foot-8 and his listed playing weight was 153. Years later Waner himself said, "My highest weight was 148 pounds.

Waner had a picture perfect swing and that's one reason that teams sought his services after his playing days to teach young hitters. Even when he was into his fifties, Waner, who died at 62, maintained his form. During one of his spring training sessions when he was tutoring St. Louis Cardinals, Waner got to reminiscing.

"I was a line-drive hitter," he said, "but one year I decided to swing for the fences. I hit 15 home runs—a lot in those days—but my batting average dropped to .336. I believe I would have led the league in hitting that year if I hadn't become home-run conscious. I decided then and there no more swinging from the heels for me."

That was 1929 and lest a listener think that it was a wasted season for Waner, he did drive in 100 runs, and as a bonus stole 15 bases.

Waner said that he always hit the New York Giants well, even though they usually had a good team and good pitching and once he and his brother Lloyd collected 15 hits between them in a doubleheader versus New York. The secret, Waner said, was that they were both excellent curve ball hitters and when John McGraw managed the Giants he showed favoritism to good curve ball pitchers. That meant good results for the Waners and the Pirates.

However, Waner's career extended far beyond the time of McGraw's retirement and when Bill Terry assumed command it became harder to feast upon Giants hurlers.

"He plastered a $25 fine on any of his pitchers who threw me a curve ball," Waner said. "Roy Parmelee threw it in our last game with the Giants. I hit it into the right-field seats."

Waner was even successful against future Hall of Famer Carl Hubbell, who specialized in a screwball. Hubbell said that Waner was the toughest foe for him to get out.

"Hub would hold the Pittsburgh club to four hits and I'd get two," Waner said.

Waner could make Hubbell a bit grumpy.

"One thing I learned," Hubbell said, "was never to throw him a slow ball. He'd hit any kind of pitch, but give him a slow ball and he'd place it on a two-bit piece in left-center or right-center, and that's kind of humiliating for the fella who's pitching."

When the Waners were growing up on the family farm, they took their amusement in the fields. The smooth way that Paul adjusted to hitting the curve dated back to the first implement he swung at in lieu of a ball.

"I have never batted a curve ball thrown by any pitcher that was as hard to hit as the cobs the boys used to throw at me down on the farm. A cob thrown hard enough just naturally takes all kind of unnatural shoots and jumps. We used a stick for a bat and played that game by the hour and we played it every day of the week. That's where I learned to follow the ball."

It was known that Paul Waner drank quite a bit and once when he arrived at the park for a Pirates game against the St. Louis Cardinals he wasn't feeling his best. He asked Cardinals catcher Gabby Street to help protect him by asking the pitcher not to throw at his head. Street said the Cardinals didn't throw at players' heads anyway, but he would tell anyone who took the mound that day.

Wouldn't you know it, but Waner smacked four doubles and was responsible for the win.

Once Waner got past his brief, early-career infatuation with hitting home runs, he realized that he was not built for that kind of work. That 15-homer year was tops for Waner, but during that MVP season he managed to knock in 131 runs with just nine home runs.

"I always have figured that it would be foolish for a player of my weight to try for home runs," Waner said. "I haven't got the power to propel the ball over the fence. I know it and try to make up for my lack of strength my using a little judgment. I try to place my hits. The opposing teams know that I don't always hit to the same field and the players have to spread out. That's just what I work for. With the fielders unable to play for a set spot, I have a good chance to find a hole for my drives."

Waner really did everything but hit home runs. He collected 191 triples, twice leading the league and once hitting as many as 22 in a season. He scored runs in bunches, too. Nine times Waner scored at least 100 runs in a season and he twice led the National League in that category. In 1928 he scored a career-high 142 runs and he led the league again in 1934 with 122 runs scored. In almost every measurable way Waner was an extraordinarily player with longevity.

He suited up for the Pirates in 2,154 games, is second on the team's all-time list for run scoring, third in hits, third in singles, leads in double, is second in triples and taking into account just his time in Pittsburgh has the highest lifetime average of anyone to ever play for the Pirates. That mark is .340.

One of the strangest aspects of Waner's career was that it was not learned for many years that he was actually near-sighted. The Pirates found out one day when Waner said something about not being able to read the extra-large signs on the outfield walls. No doubt thinking that their star hitter would be even better if he could see the ball better, they brought him to an eye doctor. Waner was tested and out-fitted with glasses, but they actually turned him into a worse hitter, so he didn't stick with them. It was difficult to make sense of that, but somehow Waner had coped for many years.

Waner, who was inducted into the Hall of Fame, in 1952, was referred to as "Big Poison" compared to Lloyd. Lloyd was actually physically larger, even if Paul was older. The story goes that the nickname derived from a Brooklyn fan that was sick of the Dodgers being pummeled by the Waner brothers.

This person supposedly referred to them as big person and little person, but in such a thick local accent that it came off as Big Poison and Little Poison. That may be true, but in terms of their hitting stature, Paul was Big Poison no matter how anyone spins it.

Waner's drinking problem was common knowledge—at least within the sport—and in 1938 team officials asked him to stop drinking. He did, although he only batted .280 that season. It was Casey Stengel, who often spoke what was perceived to be his own language, who once said of Paul Waner, "He had to be a very graceful player because he could slide without breaking the bottle on his hip."

In 2007, the Pirates retired Waner's No. 11 uniform jersey.

Courtesy of the National Baseball Hall of Fame Library

For much of the 20th century **Harold "Pie" Traynor** was considered the best third baseman of all time. A career Pirate Traynor batted .320 in his Hall of Fame career.

4
PIE TRAYNOR

For decades Harold "Pie" Traynor was pretty much considered the best third baseman in baseball history by acclamation. He was not only a vacuum cleaner with his glove, but he was the best hitting third sacker of them all. The Hall of Famer who played his entire 17-year career with the Pirates compiled a .320 lifetime average. That alone put him in special territory.

Traynor naturally enough earned his nickname because of a fondness for eating slices of pie. Born in 1898 in Framingham, Massachusetts, Traynor stood 6 feet tall and weighed about 170 pounds.

Never a big home-run hitter (he belted just 58 in his career), Traynor drove in 1,273 runs. The All-Star game was not created until he was in his mid-thirties and near the end of his playing days, but Traynor represented the National League in 1933 and 1934, the first two years the exhibition was staged.

Traynor broke into the majors in 1920 and retired following the 1937 season. He was a key member of the Pirates, however, in 1925, when they captured the World Series, and in 1927 when they won another NL pennant. Traynor's three biggest hitting years were 1930 when he batted .366, 1929 when he batted .356, and 1927 when he batted .342.

The game, hustling player was known for making timely hits. And New York Giants Hall of Fame manager John McGraw was pretty much driven crazy by Traynor's expertise in the field. McGraw summed up Traynor's game as "the best. I've never seen anything like him. I'll bet he ruined more base hits for my club than any other two infielders in the game."

Many of the finest hitters in baseball were very particular about the piece of wood they carried to home plate for their cuts. They had them made to certain specifications. They broke them in. They boned them. Traynor was a contradiction to the norm. When a Pittsburgh sportswriter once asked what kind of bat he used Traynor seemed surprised.

"Any I could pick up that pleased my fancy," Traynor said. "I stole most of them. You know how clubs lay out the bats in front of the dugouts. Well, I'd just stroll around and pick them up and try them. If I came across one I liked I'd take it. I wouldn't exactly steal it. I'd tell the manger or somebody else on the club that I was taking it. I liked to get the old ones, with the lumber well-seasoned."

Rather amazingly Traynor not only did this type of borrowing from his own teammates, but the day's opponents, as well, occasionally. He had the audacity to wander over to the foe's dugout area and check out their war clubs—and then lean down and actually take one for use in the game!

"Many a hit I made against a club with one of its own bats I'd helped myself to that way," Traynor said. "The reason I liked the old ones was that they had more oomph and drive in them."

If that is one of the strangest habits by a superior hitter, then so be it, but Traynor did not employ the same strategy with his gloves. Although listening to him describe the scruples attached to avoiding such a move it makes one speculate that he might have under different circumstances.

"You can't take another player's glove," Traynor said. "He has to buy his gloves and shoes. I used to buy about five pairs of shoes at $17 a pair, and three gloves."

Apparently that meant that everyone in the league was safe and wouldn't become another Shoeless Joe Jackson.

At least for the first 30 or more years after he retired (and maybe longer) Traynor remained the No. 1 third baseman in everyone's eyes. Brooks Robinson probably was a better fielder and in recent years the vote for the best all-around fielding and hitting third baseman has turned Mike Schmidt's way, but Traynor is on the short list for those making comparisons.

Traynor didn't even really try to hit homers.

"I was a choke-up hitter," he said of the way he gripped those bats on loan. "I always used a thick-handled bat."

Even though he was not a home-run man, Traynor played in 1,914 games, cracked 2,416 hits, and managed to drive in more than 100 runs in a season seven times. Traynor's fame was enduring around baseball and especially in Pittsburgh. In 1971, when he was well into retirement, the Pirates threw a special night and dinner for Traynor. The program was loaded with well wishes, some of the creative sort. Iron City Beer, the popular local concoction, took out an ad reading, "The No. 1 Beer Salutes the No. 1 Third Baseman." The Pittsburgh Penguins hockey team ad read this way: "Pie, The way you stopped shots at the hot corner you would have made a great goalie."

In that same program, Traynor gave away some trade secrets, more or less. The piece that ran under his name was called "How To Play Third Base." Traynor began, "Like any other player on the field, the third baseman must always make up his mind, before each pitch, exactly what to do with the ball if it is hit to him. But like a woman's mind and the cost of living, that decision is subject to change without notice." Split-second thinking is often needed, he said, and experience mattered, too.

That same year Traynor threw out the first pitch at a Pirates World Series game at Three Rivers Stadium.

A couple of years earlier, Traynor, then 70, explained to an interviewer that he had never learned to drive an automobile and walked everywhere he could.

"I never learned to drive because I was afraid I'd find an excuse not to walk," Traynor said, "which I've found so enjoyable, so relaxing and healthful."

Traynor maintained an apartment in downtown Pittsburgh that was, of course, within walking distance of Forbes Field, the place where he played his entire career. On opening day of the 1969 season Traynor set out for the park and thought about taking the bus, but when it arrived it was packed.

"I didn't push myself," he said, "but I got there before the bus."

It was a long time since anyone had called Traynor "Harold." He acquired his nickname when he was a little boy and chased balls into the woods for local players. He was often rewarded with a piece of pie. The baker saw the boy so often he called him "Pieface." He was better off that only half of the nickname stuck.

There was some irony that Traynor ended up as a lifelong Pirate. His family moved from Framingham to Somerville, even closer to downtown Boston, and a Boston Braves scout saw Traynor first. He told him he had potential and sent him to see Braves manager George Stallings at Braves Field. Only no one alerted Stallings and when Traynor showed up the skipper was in a bad mood and ran him off. Big mistake. Once installed in the Pirates lineup Traynor made Stallings and the Braves miserable many times.

Baseball as a sport was rougher around the edges when Traynor broke in and the spring training regimen really was for getting into shape after the long winter. The Pirates trained in Hot Springs, Arkansas and manager George Gibson drilled his men twice a day before the season.

"Back in the twenties we never even thought about bringing our wives or our families South with us," Traynor said. "Silent movies were about the only break in our training routine."

The famous sportswriter Red Smith said that Traynor was the first Major League player he ever met in 1928 when breaking into the journalism business for the St. Louis Star. Traynor came to town to see a friend and go on a hunting trip and the young scribe was assigned to interview him. Smith said he didn't remember anything notable Traynor said, but always recalled his friendliness. As Smith grew more experienced, though, and added some perspective to his thinking, he reached a conclusion: "Traynor was the best third baseman I ever saw."

Those who watched Traynor perform on a daily basis, or regularly during the seasons, concurred. Charlie Grimm, the long-serving Cubs employee in a variety of positions, was one of those opponents who raved about Traynor. Although it is often forgotten, Grimm broke in with the Pirates, and was a Traynor teammate.

"Traynor protected the territory around third and the left side of the mound as if he owned it," Grimm said. "Which he did. He just got everything, that's all. He was great at the plate, too, a terrific hitter. But he sure could hang out those line drives."

Traynor managed the Pirates from 1934 to 1939 and was elected to the Hall of Fame in 1948. The Pirates retired his No. 20 jersey in 1972 and he passed away that same year.

Courtesy of the National Baseball Hall of Fame Library

One of the great power hitters in history, **Ralph Kiner** set a record by leading the National League in homers seven years in a row, an achievement that earned him a place in the Hall of Fame.

5
RALPH KINER

The powerful slugger was at his best when the Pittsburgh Pirates were at their worst. When the team was terrible in the late 1940s and early 1950s Kiner gave the fans at Forbes Field something to cheer about. He was unique in that he was able to smash prodigious home runs at a higher rate than anyone he played against in the National League for years on end.

Kiner broke into the majors in 1946 and led the NL in homers for the first seven years straight of his career, an unprecedented accomplishment. He was 6-foot-2 and 195 pounds, and could hit the ball beyond barriers with startling regularity. Although he played just 10 seasons in the majors, (retiring younger than he wished because of a chronic back problem) mostly with Pittsburgh, Kiner made enough noise to gain Hall of Fame recognition.

In order, Kiner hit 23, 51, 40, 54, 47, 42 and 37 homers, with each figure leading the National League throughout the late 1940s and into the 1950s, an astounding achievement. Less publicized was the fact that Kiner drove in more than 100 runs six times, with a mostly bad team. He was chosen for six All-Star teams and led the NL in slugging percentage three times.

Although most people who saw Kiner play in person would have reached the same conclusion, Kiner made it easy for baseball fans to memorize his hitting philosophy.

"I try to hit the ball as hard as I can every time I swing," he said.

The only reason that Kiner did not play his entire career with the Pirates was money. He wanted more of it than general manager Branch Rickey was willing to pay and so Rickey traded him off to the Chicago

Cubs. Kiner came to Rickey looking for a raise based on still another league-leading home-run performance. Having grown up in California during the Great Depression, Kiner was conscious of getting every dollar he could.

But Rickey's response was legendary. In essence, he said to Kiner, that the Pirates finished last with him and they could finish last without him. Then Rickey promptly traded away the fan favorite. That ended Kiner's stay in Pittsburgh about one-quarter of the way into the 1953 season.

Kiner grew up in the era when baseball was king in the United States and kids left their homes in the mornings, headed to the nearest playground, and didn't stop playing ball all day.

"I played just about every kind of ball you could play, both organized and unorganized," Kiner said of his youth in the 1930s and 1940s. "I played pick-up games with as many kids as we could get together, seven or eight kids on a sandlot. Then later I played Saturday afternoon ball and Sunday morning ball, all semi-pro. I also played for town teams like the Alhambra Merchants, and I played American Legion ball. There was an awful lot of ball to play in Southern California in those days."

Kiner, who died at 91 in early 2014, made an impact in his games and at that time before any Major League draft, signing young players was a free-for-all between scouts. Kiner heard from several teams and he thought of committing to the New York Yankees, but someone told him that the Yankees were so good and had so many good players he might get stuck in the minors and never get out. The Pirates were the opposite. They were talent-thin and a young, promising player could make it to the big leagues much faster through the Pittsburgh chain. That did it for Kiner. Even with a $3,000 bonus that didn't make Kiner very special to teammates when he was invited to spring training. As was common at the time the veterans didn't welcome the recent high school grad very warmly because they didn't want to lose their jobs.

"The veterans wouldn't let me take batting practice," Kiner said. "I couldn't get near the batting cage. They resented the competition and kept you out."

Kiner impressed with the frequency of his home runs, but also with the distance they traveled. One of those blasts was particularly memorable. During a 1950 game at Forbes Field Kiner launched a home run over the left-field scoreboard by a margin estimated at 50 feet. Still heading into orbit as it departed the playing field, the Kiner blast shot out of the ball park and into neighboring Schenley Park, where it bounced and settled into a stand of trees. No official distance was marked off measuring how far the ball flew, but those on the scene guessed more than 550 feet. At least one theory holds that the ball did not land until it was 575 feet from home plate. That would make it one of the most prodigious home runs of all time.

Kiner got his kicks from hitting home runs and thought it was weird when others suggested that the right-handed hitting slugger should place the ball for hits to the opposite field more often.

"Here's the way I've figured it out," Kiner said. "Right-handed power hitters who hit to right drive flivvers. But the right-handed power hitters who hit to left, drive 12-cylinder limousines."

Kiner knew what he was and knew what he wanted to be. And he knew what he wanted to drive.

In the 1920s and 1930s Babe Ruth led the home-run revolution with his 60 in 1927 and players such as Jimmie Foxx and Hank Greenberg (a mentor to Kiner) also clubbed 58 homers apiece, but then a little lull hit the game and the 50-homer man was shelved for a while. Kiner brought the big blasts back and twice hit more than 50 in a season.

It took almost no time for Kiner to establish himself as the king of the dingers. Kiner, like many of his contemporaries, missed a couple of seasons of play because of World War II service as a Navy pilot and that was one reason he took people so unawares as a rookie. Even if he was going to make good, it was believed he might need some minor-league seasoning, or at the very least a refresher course to get back his timing.

Kiner became a big celebrity and in the giddy days after the war he mingled with the Hollywood crowd. He was handsome, dated starlets, and his love life found its way into gossip columns. Kiner spent a warm California night with Elizabeth Taylor which involved accompanying her to a movie premiere at Grauman's Chinese Theatre and then dining at Romanoff's, the famed restaurant. When a sportswriter asked Kiner to rate Taylor on a scale of 1-to-10, he said, "Eleven."

Kiner appeared in the movie "Angels in the Outfield" hitting a home run and while on the set he met actress Janet Leigh and they dated. Kiner also appeared on the TV shows, "What's My Line?" and "I've Got A Secret."

For a guy who did so much damage with his bat Kiner was always mild-mannered off the field. But he worked hard at his craft.

"People think being a ball player is just a two-hour-a-day job," he said, "but it isn't. You have to work at it all the time. At least I do."

Although Kiner played on losing teams in Pittsburgh he said joining the Pirates was one of the best things that ever happened to him. To some fans he just remained a name on the top of the statistics list since there were no televised national games and his club never made it into the post-season.

"I got pretty good acclaim for being buried where I was," Kiner said. "Of course, if I had been with a better ball club I probably would have received a lot more publicity. I think that probably hurt me in my election to the Hall of Fame because I didn't get that much exposure."

Kiner hit just .279 lifetime as he was piling up those power numbers. He said that when Hank Greenberg, the Detroit Tigers star, came to Pittsburgh for the last season of his career that Kiner picked up a lot of pointers that were helpful.

"I really didn't get it all together until I met Hank Greenberg," Kiner said. "He spent a lot of time working with me and this is where I really got all the instruction I ever got out of baseball."

After retiring at 33 because of his back woes (though he later wished he'd stayed on longer), Kiner hooked on in the broadcast world, first doing a post-game show for the Pirates, then with the Chicago White Sox. While also working as a Mets broadcaster, most famously Kiner hosted a lively segment called "Kiner's Korner." Kiner became known as someone who could accidentally mangle the English language in a humorous manner.

Kiner was inducted into the Baseball Hall of Fame in 1975 and in 1987 the Pirates retired his No. 4 uniform jersey.

"I should be honoring you," Kiner told Pittsburgh fans.

Courtesy of the National Baseball Hall of Fame Library

Hall of Famer **Willie Stargell** was called "Pops" as a gesture of respect late in his career and retired with 475 home runs and two Pirate World Series rings.

6
WILLIE STARGELL

His Pittsburgh teammates called Willie Stargell "Pops," and he was definitely the Papa Pirate who sat at the head of the table. He was the physical and spiritual team leader who played his way into the Hall of Fame and who inspired players who took the field near him.

In 21 years in the majors, all spent with the Pirates, the lefty swinging Stargell smacked 475 home runs, was a seven-time All-Star, notched five 100 RBI seasons, and was the heart and soul of the 1979 Pittsburgh World Series champions.

That year, Stargell, who also played for the 1971 Series winners, won the Most Valuable Player award. Coming as it did 19 seasons into a career that began with the Pirates in 1962 it was the culmination of his contributions to the franchise. One of the most popular players in Pittsburgh and within the team, the 6-foot-2, 200-pound Stargell often seemed bigger than life. He was so strong he hit seven balls out of Forbes Field, which happened just 16 times in all.

Stargell was not usually categorized as a pure slugger, but could still powder home runs in bunches. When he went on one of his flurries it sometimes provoked sportswriters into asking if he felt he could top Babe Ruth or Roger Maris and their 60-homer seasons. In reality, Stargell never topped 50.

Yet he did capture two National League home-run crowns, smacking 48 in 1971 and 44 in 1973.

"You can't think home run when you go up there," Stargell said. "You have to go up there thinking about the pitcher and what he's going to throw you. And you have to think about the situation at the time. You can't go up there with anything like a Babe Ruth on your mind."

Stargell was respected among his peers and he was liked by the community. He was a player whose good nature transcended the field and he got involved in charitable causes. One group he helped was a fund-raising arm for research for the cure of Sicklecell anemia.

"Wherever I go to speak, I ask people to make a contribution rather than take a fee," he said.

Stargell first appeared in the Bucs lineup in 1962 for 10 games. He last played for Pittsburgh in 1982. He grew up and he grew athletically old with the team. Besides blistering those home runs, Stargell always knocked in his share of runs. He accumulated 1,540 RBIs during his career and he led the National League by knocking in 119 runs 1973.

Although he made his mark in a Pirates uniform soon after putting it on for the first time, Stargell was not a cocky player, and it took him a few years to feel as if he really belonged in the majors. It was a pinch-me-to-see-if-it-is-real time for him. At one point during the 1966 season Stargell stroked nine straight hits and that seemed to be a mistake.

"This can't be happening to me," Stargell said. "I can understand Roberto Clemente getting nine hits in a row, but not Willie Stargell." But Stargell was becoming a Roberto Clemente-type player.

Stargell's lifetime average was .282 and he wasn't a threat to win a batting title, but he was always a threat to win a game when he stepped into the batter's box. The secret to good hitting, he said in a 1974 interview, was being able to adjust.

"Every pitcher throws totally unlike another one," he said, "so I think the ability of the individual, I'm talking about the hitter, to adjust, in given situations, where if he's a good fastball hitter, and there's a good curve ball hitter, it's not a matter of guessing what the pitcher is going to throw. You have to know exactly what he's going to throw."

Stargell had many good seasons, but 1979 was the pinnacle of his career in the way it combined team and individual success and the manner in which the older player helped carry and cajole the young players to the World Series championship. Stargell was 38 and only two seasons earlier he had incurred so many injuries, to his back, knees, legs and arm, that there was speculation he was going to have to retire. Then he won the NL Comeback Player of the Year award in 1978 and came all of the way back the next season.

"This is not an 'I' game, it's 'We,'" Stargell said. "There's no one man who dominates any game. When I've lost my desire and enthusiasm for this game, I'll step aside for a younger player."

Actually, things went so well for Stargell and the Pirates in 1979 that he could joke in the locker room even after he made an error, throwing the ball 10 feet over the head of third baseman Bill Madlock. Invoking the popular Steelers football star of the time, Stargell said, "I showed people that Terry Bradshaw isn't the only one who can throw a down-and-out pass in this town."

In the World Series against Baltimore Stargell hit three home runs, drove in seven, and batted .400. He looked younger by the game, which may be why he also was chosen as MVP of the Series.

Referring to the season as a whole, as well as the championship, Madlock said of Stargell's leadership, "Willie wouldn't let us die."

That was what he seemed destined to do in that shining season. Manager Chuck Tanner said that the other players looked to Stargell for guidance and leadership in every way all season long, saying, "C'mon Pops, lead the way, get us out of here." Stargell's continuing advice all year long, especially to the younger players who might be more prone to nervousness, was to "have fun."

This was the season more than any other that the Pirates emphasized the theme of family. Yet the roster was probably the most diverse in the game, with them all pulling together for the same cause.

"We have shown what men can do together," Stargell said. "We have blacks, whites, Latins, but we were family. We had to scratch and crawl sometimes, but we did it together."

Accolades accumulated for Stargell, seemingly even more for what type of person he was than what type of hitter he was.

"I've been with him eight years," said infielder Rennie Stennett. "You have a problem, you're at your lowest, you talk to Willie. A baseball problem, or anything. He is a man you can trust, a man you know will help."

The 1979 season was essentially Stargell's last hurrah. He hung on for three more years, into his forties, but played in just 67, 38, and 74 games, injuries eventually running him out of the sport.

Stargell knew the time had come and he announced his retirement leading up to the end of the 1982 season. He was also plotting his future. He said he was memorizing speeches by Dr. Martin Luther King Jr. and was going to speak them to a live audience accompanied by the Eastman School Philharmonic of Rochester, New York. He did emphasize, rather strongly, "But I won't be singing." That was apparently for the benefit of anyone who believed he could do anything.

The body showing its age at 41 was what Stargell said let him know it was time to hang up his Pirates uniform.

"It's time for me to step aside and let some kids take over," Stargell said. "I feel I've competed enough. The knees have had it. You have only so many miles in them and I think mine have gone 50,000 miles."

Stargell talked of a vacation to France, possible broadcast work, maybe someday managing, but he sounded like a contented man, satisfied with what he had done in the sport. In 1988 Stargell was voted into the Hall of Fame. He was chosen the first time he was on the ballot with more than 82 percent of the vote.

When notified, Stargell, who was then living in Stone Mountain,

Georgia, admitted that he teared up at the enormity of the honor.

"I've lost that big ol composure," Stargell said. "To be in the same room as Babe (Ruth), Hank (Aaron), and Ernie (Banks)," he said. "What a feeling! What an honor! Just the words 'Hall of Fame' give me chills. It's almost impossible to think it could happen to you. All that hard work and sacrifice, I never thought it would feel like this. I never thought I would have a day like this. I'm overwhelmed."

Another thing that Stargell didn't see coming and which put more than 50,000 miles on his body was a kidney ailment which debilitated and led to his death at only 61 in 2001. Only days before Stargell's death the Pirates moved into PNC Park and unveiled a 12-foot high statue of "Pops." He was too ill to attend.

"When you had Willie Stargell on your team," Tanner said, "it was like having a diamond ring on your finger."

Courtesy of the National Baseball Hall of Fame Library

Shortstop **Arky Vaughan** was a brilliant bat wielder, winning a batting title and hitting .318 on his way to the Hall of Fame.

7
ARKY VAUGHAN

A self-made shortstop and third baseman through hard work and a wizard with the bat, Arky Vaughan played 14 years in the big leagues, and most of the best ones were the 10 seasons he spent with the Pittsburgh Pirates from the time he broke in for the 1932 season until he was traded to the Brooklyn Dodgers.

Vaughan was a nine-time All-Star with a .318 lifetime batting average who led the National League in triples three times, three times topped the circuit in runs batted in, and most significantly led the NL in batting with a .385 average in 1935.

Born in Emoryville, California in 1912, Vaughan was a lefty swinger. He stood 5-foot-10 and weighed 175 pounds. Vaughan wasn't normally a big home-run hitter, but one season he did belt 19.

Vaughan's given name was Joseph Floyd and until he picked up his nickname while still in California, he was better known as Floyd. Definitely one of the Pirates' all-time greats, Vaughan nearly became a New York Yankee. The Yankee scout in California knew of Vaughan, but he also had to check out a pitcher. On a given day both Vaughan and the other young were playing some distance apart. The scout chose to attend the pitcher's ballgame and as a result he was beaten to Vaughan by the Pirates scout.

Pittsburgh's scout on the scene was Art Griggs and he took his seat in the grandstand to watch the game being played in the town of Cypress, California, near Fullerton where Vaughan attended high school. The best professional scouts always trust their instincts, certainly as much as the numbers such as those measuring a pitcher's velocity. In this case Vaughan was the shortstop on the field and time after time in the early going his range, throws and glove work brought him attention.

That's what endeared Vaughan to Griggs and he became a Pirate.

Vaughan was only 23 when he captured that batting title and that earned him a certain notoriety around the league, especially since his final mark was within hailing distance of .400. A minor injury that sidelined him briefly may have cost him his best shot at that magic number.

One person who took note of Vaughan's potential was that great Pirate star Honus Wagner, who had led the National League in hitting eight times himself.

"See the kid out there?" Wagner said, pointing to Vaughan on the field. "Some kid, eh? He's one of the sweetest hitters I ever saw. And fast! They don't make 'em any faster. He's improved a lot as a fielder, too. I get a great kick out of watching the kid."

If Vaughan wanted anyone in the Pirates organization to notice him and compliment him so lavishly, no better source could be uncovered.

Vaughan kept on improving his fielding, too, until he ranked among the best in the sport at scooping up ground balls and throwing runners out at first. He had learning pains and one year committed 46 errors, but he smoothed over his work. It was said he was in slow motion when chasing grounders at first, but when his judgment became savvier and he played lighter on his feet he became slicker with the glove.

One Pirate manager who made a big impression on Vaughan was Frank Frisch. After his playing days as a Hall of Fame second baseman for the New York Giants and the St. Louis Cardinals, Frisch took over the Bucs. As a hustling player who played with grit, Frisch did not like to even sense fielders appearing slightly lazy in the field.

Vaughan remembered Frisch arriving on the scene and taking charge of the infield, where he was most at home.

"Grab that ball and fire it!" Frisch said. "Turn it loose. Show a little fire—or else."

At that moment the Pirates infield consisted of Elbie Fletcher at first base, second baseman Frankie Gustine, Lee Handley on third and Vaughan playing short. Gustine was just up from the minors and was gung-ho to make a positive impression.

"But Gustine was too ambitious," Vaughan said. "Frankie took a throw from Fletcher, turned, and opened fire on me at about 30 feet. He threw that thing with all he had. I caught it on the index finger of my right hand, my throwing fist. I guess what I called Gustine then was pretty unreasonable."

The throw broke Vaughan's finger. The trainer looked over the injury and placed it in a splint. Vaughan stayed around and came to bat with his finger sticking straight out in the air as he tried to wrap his hands around the handle. Vaughan was frustrated and angry—until he swung and connected.

"I had one of the greatest hitting streaks of my career," Vaughan said. "They just couldn't get me out. I hit line drives to all fields."

The peculiar protective contraption made him concentrate all of the more apparently. But strangely, as soon as the finger healed and the splint came off, Vaughan went into a slump. Slumps were not common for Vaughan. Although the .385 was his highest average, during his decade with the Pirates Vaughan batted over .300 every year.

Vaughan had a somewhat awkward hitting style, one that a Giants player once ridiculed by saying that one day Vaughan would "rupture" himself swinging so hard. But Hughie Critz, another Giants player, overheard and said, "He's already ruptured me trying to get in front of those balls he hits to right field."

It wasn't just his averages that were impressive. Vaughan had a knack for getting on base one way or the other. He had three straight seasons with phenomenal on-base percentages in the mid-1930s. In 1934 his mark was .434. The next year Vaughan reached base at a rate of .491. Pitchers pretty much had to close up shop against him that season. Then in 1936 he reached at a pace of .453. He could be a valuable man in the lineup.

As he became a seasoned veteran Vaughan thought he detected a trend among young players that was not a good thing for the future of the fielding profession.

"They all want to throw and hit," he said in a kids-today monologue. "But they shy away from accepting a hot grounder. It can be dangerous. A bad hop can knock you cold. I shouldn't talk. I wasn't a graceful fielder. No one ever accused me of being a leather man."

Vaughan brought up a point on the manner in which infielders tended to warm up which may still be valid today. Why should they lob the ball back and forth in the air for a light game of catch like a father and son playing in the backyard?

"The whole training system is wrong," Vaughan said. "…they could profit from throwing the ball on the ground in their warm-ups."

Young fielders need more encouragement, Vaughan said, because it is basically what would be called politically incorrect to admit that they are afraid of a batted ball when in reality the inner fear may be there and must be worked out for success.

"It takes more guts to go down on a hard-hit grounder than it does to stand up to a fastball pitcher," Vaughan said. "I've done both. Don't back away from the ball. Make it come to you. Play it on the big hop. Be aggressive. Move in on a grounder before it has a chance to intimidate you on the off hop. But don't fight it. The big thing is to stoop low."

Vaughan very much did sound like someone who had been there.

Besides excelling at baseball, Vaughan was a true blue outdoorsman who was devoted to fishing and hunting. At the end of each baseball season he and some teammates embarked for Wyoming to go hunting. Vaughan was traded to Brooklyn for four players in 1941 and played four seasons with the Dodgers, though his time was interrupted by military service.

Vaughan was at least as active as ever indulging his outdoor hobbies in retirement. However, that enthusiasm ultimately cost him his life.

Vaughan was on a fishing trip when the boat overturned on August 30, 1952 and he perished at age 40. He was fishing on Lost Lake in California with a friend who also drowned in the same mishap. There were witnesses when the boat tipped over and threw them into the lake and they began swimming to shore.

They were perhaps 65 feet from land when the incident began, but went under the cold water and didn't surface after they reached within about 20 feet of shore. The lake, inside an extinct volcano, was estimated to be about 2,000 feet deep, and it remains deep all of the way up to the shore, so the men would have been unable to stand up and walk at all before reaching land. Their bodies were not recovered until the next day.

Courtesy of the National Baseball Hall of Fame Library

Some say that Hall of Famer **Bill Mazeroski** was the best fielding second baseman in history, but Mazeroski gained greater fame for smacking the World Series-winning home run to beat the Yankees in 1960.

8
BILL MAZEROSKI

The home run will be in the lead sentence of Bill Mazeroski's obituary. Although he often wishes someone would talk about something else, it is inevitable. The man who connected for the most dramatic hit in baseball history is stuck with his accomplishment as a lifetime tag. At least it is something to be proud of rather than being followed around for decades by something one would be ashamed of doing.

In 1960 Mazeroski hit a home run in the ninth inning to give the Pittsburgh Pirates a World Series championship over the New York Yankees that just didn't figure. Although he accomplished many other things in his long Major League baseball career Mazeroski ensured a kind of immortality with his blow.

Winning the seventh game of the World Series on a home run is every Little League player's fantasy, every Major League player's fantasy. It is indeed the stuff of dreams. Of course there was much more to Mazeroski the man, and Mazeroski the ball player. If there had not been he would not have been elected to the Hall of Fame. That was the sum of his career, but if he had only hit the home run that would have been enough for baseball fans in Pittsburgh.

While feted and hailed for decades because of the remarkable timing of his big hit, Mazeroski hated to be singled out from that extraordinary championship team. Once, when the advertising was being formulated for a Pirates fantasy camp, he got wind that it was going to be billed as "Bill Mazeroski and the '60 Bucs." He was a guy who recognized the value of team and shunned that label.

"It's not about that," Mazeroski said. "It's about the '60 Bucs. I was just part of it. I got one lucky hit. I get too much credit. It took a 25-

man team to win and I was just a very, very small part of it."

There is truth in what Mazeroski says and there is too much self-deprecation in what he says. Everyone knows teams win games and championships, but on that day he was the headliner. Somebody had to hit the ball deep off of Yankees pitcher Ralph Terry or else the trophy doesn't go to the Pirates.

It takes more than one huge hit or one magnificent season to be elected to the Hall of Fame. The son of a coal miner, Mazeroski was born in Wheeling, West Virginia in 1936, but grew up in a small town in Ohio and spent his entire 17-year career with the Pirates between 1956 and 1972. Mazeroski was a seven-time All-Star and won eight Gold Gloves and many think of him as the finest fielding second baseman in history.

With the exception of the memorable home run in the 1960 Series, Mazeroski was always better known for his glove work than his bat work. His lifetime batting average was .260. Mazeroski clouted 138 home runs in his career and never topped 100 runs scored or 100 RBIs in a season. What he did mostly was prevent the other team from scoring.

One thing about Mazeroski was that he was ever-popular with Pittsburgh fans. He may not ever have hit in the same league as Honus Wagner, Paul Waner or Roberto Clemente, but he was a hit with the people. In 1999 a fan vote was taken to choose a Pirates All-Century team and not only was Mazeroski selected as the second baseman on that mythical club he received more votes than any other single player.

In those pre-Internet days there were slightly more than 14,000 votes cast and Mazeroski received 13,049 worth.

"It's hard to believe," Mazeroski said. "It's a tremendous honor that I could get more votes than Honus Wagner, Pie Traynor, Ralph Kiner and Roberto Clemente.

Not every position had the same level of competition. Whereas

Clemente was head-to-head with Paul Waner in right field, two Hall of Famers, the same depth was not evident at each position.

Mazeroski led with his glove and his spirit. Players who came along in the 20th century always wondered how their predecessors could field with the small gloves they used before the leather was shaped better and higher quality, larger gloves came into regular use. Mazeroski, much like his forebears, always used a smaller glove.

"It's small, all right," he admitted, "and the manufacturers quit making the model years ago. But I can field a ball quicker and the ball doesn't get lost in the glove when I want to throw. I have small hands, you know."

When he discovered that his favorite glove was going to be discontinued, Mazeroski bought five at once so he wouldn't run out. He didn't want to break his habit of using the same model for as long as he could put it off. Some might call that superstition, but for Maz it just meant that he didn't want to tamper with success.

Not only teammates and those in the Pirates organization that saw him play every day admired Mazeroski's style in the field. So did opponents.

"I've been around for more than 40 years and I've never seen a better second baseman," said Johnny Pesky, the long-time Boston Red Sox player and coach. "I've never seen a faster hand on the double play to first base."

He liked to play in every game and if he was held out for a rest, or was otherwise consigned to the bench, he was a restless spectator. When manager Danny Murtaugh took Mazeroski out of a game for a few innings he hated it and made other players stuck in the dugout with him edgy.

"That's a terrible place to watch a game," Mazeroski said. "It makes me nervous. I chew tobacco, then gum. I can't understand how some players don't mind being benched. It would make a wreck out of me."

In some of the later years of his career Mazeroski seemed to have difficulty keeping his average up. Some slumps lasted a bit longer. Part of it was attributed to weight gain. Manager Larry Shepard and hitting coach Bill Virdon, an old teammate, felt he had lost his groove.

"Maz got into some bad batting habits," Virdon said. "He was swinging with one hand a lot of times."

The juice seemed to run out and Mazeroski had a couple of back-to-back .229 seasons. He lamented that he might have hit more home runs over time if he had changed his approach much earlier.

"I was never a power hitter," Mazeroski said, "but I feel I could have hit more home runs if I hadn't been trying to experiment with hitting the ball to all fields. I hit 19 homers my third year up in 1958 and my average only slipped eight points."

Every October 13 Pirates fans celebrate Mazeroski's Game 7 home run in some fashion commemorating the 10-9 victory over New York. Whatever he was doing that day Mazeroski was reminded of it. It should be noted that such occurrences were not limited to the anniversary date, either.

"Most of the people tell me they won money on my homer or they lost money on it," Mazeroski said. "People tell me where they were when I hit the homer. Most of the fellows say they were working or in a bar watching the game on television. The women tell me what they were cooking that day, or where they were sitting. I guess it's nice that they remember me for something. The thing that gets me is that defense—in general—rarely is recognized."

Mazeroski is one of those players who would have loved to play forever, but he realized when his time was up after the 1972 season.

"I would rather be remembered for my fielding," he said. "But it can't be. That home run was the greatest thrill of my baseball life, but I don't think I'll ever go down as a great hitter. When I started playing the game I wanted to be a complete ball player. You can't live on one hit. I had 13 more years to play in the big leagues. It was just another home run."

Mazeroski is the only one who thinks that.

Mazeroski led the National League in double plays for eight straight years. He held the league record for chances accepted, putouts, games and assists by a second baseman. Certainly the home run helped since it was such an indelible play, but Mazeroski's fielding is what got him into the Hall of Fame by vote of the Veterans Committee in 2001, nearly 30 years after he retired.

Mazeroski accepted another honor that shocked him in 2010. The Pirates announced the erection of a statue of Mazeroski at PNC Park.

"I couldn't believe it when I first heard about it," Mazeroski said. "I just said, 'Holy cow, this can't be happening.' There have been so many great things happen to me. I don't know which one is the greatest."

"Where you been?" Paul asked Lloyd. "Chasing down the last ball Babe Ruth hit in the Series," Lloyd responded.

– Lloyd Waner

9
LLOYD WANER

It was almost as if Lloyd Waner was allergic to home runs. It seemed nearly impossible for such a good hitter to avoid hitting home runs. But Waner managed to bat .316 over an 18-year career, all but the last few years with the Pirates, and bash just 27 home runs. One might have figured that sticking the bat out and connecting by accident he would have accumulated more.

The younger brother of Paul Waner, Lloyd Waner was also born in Harrah, Oklahoma. A left-handed batter and a right-handed thrower, the 5-foot-9, 150-pound half of the Waner brother duo was not a large guy, but he made his mark with his all-around hitting. Like Paul, Lloyd learned to hit by swinging at thrown corncobs.

Unlike Paul, who won batting championships, the younger Waner was not a regular All-Star, but made just one appearance after the game was founded during his career. He patrolled the outfield next to Paul and he did follow him into the Hall of Fame.

Waner broke in with the Pirates in 1927, just in time to be a member of the National League pennant-winning club that season. He batted .355 as a rookie and that was the first of 10 times Waner topped .300 in a full season (he did a couple of additional times in short seasons, as well). That year Waner collected 223 hits, a rookie record. Of those, 198 were singles.

Lloyd was really an old-style hitter, a deadball era-type of hitter, playing in the new lively ball period. He accumulated 118 triples in comparison to that limited home-run total and led the National League in three-baggers in 1929 with 20. He also led the NL in hits with 214 in 1931.

One thing that made Waner so valuable to the Pirates was his ability to get on base and put himself in position to be driven in. Nine times Waner recorded an on-base percentage of .400 or more and in 1929 his on-base mark was an impressive .479.

Because he was younger, Lloyd was nicknamed "Little Poison," although he was slightly bigger than his slenderly-built older brother, who was called "Big Poison." Either way they were poisonous to opposing teams when they came to the plate. Paul totaled 3,152 hits and Lloyd had 2,459. Their combined total of 5,611 hits is a Major League record for brothers. Those closest to them are groups that included three brothers, the Alou family and the DiMaggios.

Long after both retired and passed away, Bob Broeg, the noted St. Louis sportswriter speculated that the hitters would have fallen in love with the artificial turf surfaces that popped up in the 1970s. As Hall of Fame pitcher Carl Hubbell said, "They killed you with jillions of doubles and triples."

Interestingly, Hubbell and the Waners were all from Oklahoma and knew one another, but with baseball's strict rules against fraternizing with players on other teams, Lloyd said he never went out to dinner with Hubbell when the Pirates played against the Giants.

"We weren't allowed to talk to the opposition in those days," Waner said. For the most part, though, Waner believed baseball was the same years later as when he played. "There's still a round ball and bat."

Broeg could envision balls batted by the Waners bouncing like basketballs on the hard turf and rolling to the wall as they scampered around the bases. He said one or another of them would have hit .400 if they played on artificial turf.

Although three years separated the brothers, many remarked that they resembled twins. They grew up on a farm and the grass and crops were far from artificial. They both handled the bat brilliantly and one reason Lloyd had such steady on-base percentages was that he hardly struck out, averaging one K for every 45 at-bats.

Paul was the partying brother who drank. Lloyd preferred milk. After the 1927 World Series the Waners went into vaudeville together. They wore their Pirates uniforms on stage as they did a skit that made light of losing the Series to the Yankees.

"Where you been?" Paul asked Lloyd. "Chasing down the last ball Babe Ruth hit in the Series," Lloyd responded.

Show business careers did not beckon.

"We were better ball players than we were vaudevillians," Lloyd said.

One story about the 1927 Series always rankled Pittsburgh players. It was told that they came out of the clubhouse early and watched the Yankees of that "Murderers Row" team bash ball after ball into the stands during batting practice the day before the first game and became intimidated. Irritated is more like the word that comes to mind when those Pirates talk about that. They say no such thing happened.

"If any players on our Pittsburgh club saw the Yankees hitting, I don't know who they could have been," Lloyd said. "We had worked out earlier and I saw most of the fellows leave the clubhouse and go right home. I know I did, and so did my brother Paul."

The Yankees of 1927 have often been mentioned as the greatest, or one of the greatest teams of all time, so there was no shame in losing to them, which the Pirates did.

"We gave them a battle," Lloyd Waner said. "Of course, those Yanks of '27 were the greatest ball team I ever saw. They had everything."

Long into retirement, Waner owned a home in Oklahoma where the basement was virtually a shrine to baseball. The walls were covered with photographs of him and Paul in their playing days and other stars they knew.

"I get kind of a kick out of looking at all of 'em," Waner said.

Waner appreciated one photo that Honus Wagner gave him and he saved more tangible souvenirs from games he played. Given how rarely he hit them it seemed no surprise that Waner had at least one ball of honor representing a homer. A ball resided in a glass case that was the first one he hit, versus the Boston Braves. Brother Paul wrote a note on it saying, "This ball was well hit."

It was amusing to mull Broeg's observation matching the Waner brothers and artificial turf because the way Lloyd remembered things games were played on pretty rough infields that in no way resemble the manicured lawns of the 2000s.

"They take care of 'em better," Waner said of latter era field operatives. "At Pittsburgh, and later, when I was at Boston, football would be played there late in the (baseball) season and nobody ever did anything to 'em after the games. Lots of times I'd go out early in the morning and get me a rake and try to smooth up the outfield a bit."

That meant Waner was really groundskeeper/outfielder for the Pirates.

Waner was a star with the Pirates, but during the first half of the 1940s he merely played out the string with a handful of teams, including the Phillies, Braves, Reds and Dodgers. His election to the Hall of Fame was a long time coming. His selection was not announced until 1967. He was surprised but quite pleased.

"This is a great honor and a thrill I'll live with for many years," Waner said. "I just wish Paul were alive to share this moment with me. He always said I should be in the Hall of Fame. I'm simply overwhelmed because I didn't even know I was being considered."

Paul Waner died two years earlier. One reason Waner was so surprised was that the announcement of his selection was made in Pittsburgh at the annual Dapper Dan sports banquet. He had no idea that he would be one of the hits of the night.

The person who actually presented Lloyd with his plaque was former Pirate teammate and Hall of Famer Pie Traynor.

"As much as I liked Paul Waner," Traynor said, "I always thought Lloyd lived and played under Paul's shadow. He should have been in the Hall of Fame a long time ago, but I'm happy he wasn't forgotten. He was extremely fast, probably the fastest man going to first base in the league."

To whatever degree that Lloyd was overshadowed by Paul he never indicated that it bothered him at all and looked at the situation from a different vantage point.

"It was Paul who got me a trial with the Pirates," Lloyd said. "If it hadn't been for him I wouldn't have had the opportunity, and if it hadn't been for his encouragement, I never would have lasted. He taught me a great deal."

Paul wrangled Lloyd a tryout with Pittsburgh manager Bill McKechnie, who described him as being not "much bigger than a mosquito," but someone who could play.

Lloyd Waner went into the Hall of Fame along with Branch Rickey, the executive who signed Jackie Robinson to break the color line in baseball.

Waner lived to 76 and he was in an Oklahoma hospital when he died. His long-term battle with emphysema culminated in pneumonia.

Courtesy of the National Baseball Hall of Fame Library

Max Carey was an early Pirates star who was brilliant on the bases, stealing 738 during his Hall of Fame career and leading the National League in thefts 10 times.

10
MAX CAREY

During his 19-year career, mostly spent with the Pirates, outfielder Max Carey was the finest base stealer in the National League. The future Hall of Famer stole 738 bases between 1910 and 1929 and he 10 times led the league in thefts.

Six times Carey stole more than 50 bases in a season, with a high of 63 in 1916. It was Carey's tremendous talents on the bases that made his reputation. Concurrent with his ability to swipe bases Carey five times scored at least 100 runs in a campaign. Ironically, the one season that he led the NL, Carey scored 99 times.

One of those seasons when Carey led the NL in steals he was safe 51 times in 53 tries.

Carey stood 5-foot-11 and weighed 170 pounds and he had inordinate speed. Carey was a member of the Pittsburgh pennant winner in 1925, but was traded to Brooklyn part-way through the 1927 season, so wasn't a member of the '27 NL champs. Carey did win a World Series ring with the 1925 group. Carey hit over .300 six times and was at his best during that 1925 championship season when he batted a career high .343. Not surprisingly given his skills, Carey was usually the Pittsburgh lead-off hitter. His lifetime average was .285.

In the '25 Series Carey's biggest contribution on the big stage came in the seventh game. He cracked four hits as the Pirates captured the title and batted .458 overall in the Series. In a regular-season game in 1922, one that lasted 18 innings, Carey stepped into the batter's box nine times and reached base all nine of them. He collected six hits and was walked three times that day. As was his usual habit, as long as Carey was on base that often he stole three bases. One of those was a theft of home.

Many years later Carey revealed one of the secrets that the Pirates employed in the 1925 Series when they faced the Washington Senators and ace Walter Johnson. Pittsburgh trailed the Senators 3-1 in games when Detroit Tigers star Bobby Veach got into a taxi cab with Pirates coach Jack Onslow and started chatting. Veach said, "The best way to hit Johnson, if anyone can, is to watch his delivery. When Walt rears back with his right arm, he's going to throw his fastball, which travels like a bullet. When he stops halfway, it's sure to be a curve."

Pittsburgh won the next two games and Johnson, one of the greatest hurlers of all time, was tabbed to pitch the seventh game. Employing the strategy passed on from Onslow, the Pirates beat Johnson.Carey had four hits in that game.

Not a home-run hitter, Carey spent a fair amount of his career playing in the deadball era, and excelled at collecting triples. He led the NL with 19 in 1923. Born in 1890 in Terre Haute, Indiana, Carey was just 20 when he made his big-league debut in two games with the Pirates in 1910.

When he was a young man Carey actually had an alternative career in mind. He was enrolled at Concordia College in Fort Wayne, Indiana and then signed on for courses at Concordia Seminary in St. Louis, where his plan was to study to become a minister. He attended a Central League baseball game in 1909 and that got him thinking about the sport.

"Chance plays pranks with all our lives," Carey said. "I was home for the summer vacation with the folks in Terre Haute, out of a job and with time hanging heavily on my hands. At that time I was a shortstop and pitcher. South Bend had one glaring weakness and that was at short."

Carey was highly critical of that team's new shortstop, who was subbing for a player who had advanced in the game and throughout the game he said, "'If I couldn't do better than that, I'd play for nothing.'

The idea of applying for the job fizzed itself in my mind."

Carey was so sure of himself that he was going to follow the South Bend manager into the clubhouse after the game and try to sell himself as a prospect. However, he said later that he lost his nerve. Taking the edge off his brazenness was one thing, yet giving up on the idea altogether was different. Carey instead followed the team back to its hotel and presented his case. Next thing Carey knew he was a ball player.

Initially, the boss wanted to know how fast Carey was. He happened to have captured a sprint championship and won a medal. Although Carey returned to the seminary that off-season, he returned to the ball club at the beginning of the 1910 season. In the meantime the team had rounded up another shortstop. The fresh plan was to give Carey a shot at a spot in the outfield.

"Go out to left and see what you can do," said new manager Eddie Wheeler.

Carey showed he could do pretty well as an outfielder and that became his new calling. It took only until August of that summer of 1910 before Carey was scouted and signed by the Pirates.

The player who would become famous as Max Carey was actually named Maximillian Carnarius and was the son of a minister. His parents planned all along that he would also follow that career path.

"I fully intended to conform to the wishes of my parents," Carey said, "but I became convinced that I would never be a success as a preacher and that it would be a mistake for me to take up that line of work."

From semi-pro in Indiana to Major League professional in Pittsburgh was just a short hop for Carey, who did indeed discover a line of work that he was good at. He was good enough at the sport he concentrated on rather late to become a successful switch-hitter. He threw right-handed in the field.

When Carey was in his prime as a player reporters didn't spend much time talking to the guys after games, but players were often invited to write down their thoughts in bylined stories for newspapers or magazines. Carey shared many of his habits and offered his best advice in such a column once.

A critical suggestion from Carey was that a ball player should make sure he was perceived as a team player, not an "individualist. The history of baseball has recorded numerous ball clubs with an array of outstanding individual players who have failed because they did not pull together or better—because they were not team players."

Why would anyone do this, just play for himself?

"Folks," Carey said, "there is just one answer—selfishness. Stupid, dumb, narrow-minded, self-profiting, self-asserting egotism. In baseball, as in other vocations this self-absorbing monster raises its head to demand the spotlight."

Very much conscious of the possible bad apple that could disrupt chemistry (it seemed as if Carey might have lived through such a situation), he did say that avoiding those types of players was integral to a "winning recipe. To establish and keep that winning system and team play on your club, squelch that dissenter and dumb 'smart' guy on your club and make him go along and pull with the club or else."

Carey played with and against innumerable Hall of Famers, but was not invited to join that exclusive club until long after he retired. He was selected for the Hall by the Veterans Committee in 1961. Carey was still living at age 71—in Florida at the time—so was able to enjoy the announcement.

"You've no idea of the prestige and the honor this means to me," Carey said upon being informed. "It really overwhelms me because my phone hasn't stopped ringing. Although I coveted the honor for years I never realized the importance attached to being voted into the Hall of Fame. You can play on pennant winners and world champions, but being named to the Hall of Fame comes only once in a lifetime.

I'm deeply grateful."

Once selected to the Hall Carey was showered with fresh attention and his accomplishments were extolled and revisited in newspapers across the country. So was the story of his brief managing career with the Brooklyn Dodgers. Carey hired Casey Stengel as a coach and the team decided it liked the idea of Stengel as the boss better than Carey. Carey joked that he was the only manager he knew of getting fired for losing the pennant over the winter.

Of course Carey was a Hall selectee because of his playing. Carey noted that there had never been a perfect player and that even some talented players sometimes had a year or two in the limelight and then faded. The great ones carried on, kept themselves in top shape, and never stopped working.

"Ty Cobb reached the heights through hard work, study, and application," Carey said.

Carey was 86 when he passed away in 1976.

Courtesy of the National Baseball Hall of Fame Library

Barry Bonds became baseball's all-time home-run king eventually, but he broke into the majors with the Pirates and won two Most Valuable Player awards for Pittsburgh.

11
BARRY BONDS

There was a time when Barry Bonds was loved in Pittsburgh—and he deserved it. That was so long ago not everyone will remember the 1980s and early 1990s Bonds, who was probably the most electrifying young player in the game at the time.

Bonds, who ultimately became baseball's all-time leading career home-run hitter and also became embroiled in the steroids issue, broke into the majors with Pittsburgh in 1986 and played his first seven seasons as a Pirate. Although he will be best remembered for his years with the San Francisco Giants, in Pittsburgh Bonds already made it clear that he was an extraordinary talent who would excel at bat and in the field. He was at least a four-tool player—maybe not always a great thrower.

Young Barry, the son of former All-Star Bobby Bonds, was as great a prospect as would come down the pike. Bonds was a two-time All-Star with the Pirates, won three Gold Gloves, and was a two-time National League Most Valuable Player. Then he departed from the Steel City for incredible riches as a free agent, making millions upon millions of dollars with the Giants as his reputation grew.

Bonds had a fairly non-descript rookie year, batting .223, but stole 32 bases and hit 16 homers. It was a hint of what was to come. There was improvement his second year, with 25 homers and a batting average 40 points higher. He was still a raw player with great expectations on his shoulders. He had great confidence and instincts and that may have shown up first in the field.

"I play a shallow center field because I believe if it stays in the park I can run it down," Bonds said during his second season. He said he knew that some top hitters like Eric Davis and Darryl Strawberry glanced at where he was playing them and took it as a challenge. "But I'm playing little games out there, too," Bonds added. "I'm saying under my breath, 'You can't hit a ball over my head. If you think you can, prove it to me.'"

An All-American at Arizona State, Bonds was not slated to play in the majors his rookie year, but injuries with the big club caused Pittsburgh to bring him up a year early. It is intriguing that later in his career Bonds was sometimes perceived as a selfish player, but as a young player he was looked at in the opposite fashion.

"I'm not a selfish person," Bonds said during the first month of the 1987 season. "I'm not a person who thinks for himself. Barry Bonds plays for a team, an organization. I have always been taught to play for the pride of our team, our school. Now I'm in Pittsburgh and I play for the pride of my city. That's the most important thing. We are not losers. We may have lost, but we are not losers, no more than I am a .223 hitter. We're young. We're getting better."

It took until Bonds' fourth season for him to hit .300 when he reached .301. He also batted .311 for Pittsburgh. Eventually, in his 22 years of Major League play Bonds won two batting titles and finished with a career .298 average. Although it is a statistic that doesn't get as much attention as the power numbers, Bonds led the NL in on-base percentage 10 times, including posting some astonishing figures such as .582 and .609. That was in good part because he also set the all-time big-league record for walks with 2,558.

Of course there were really a couple of different Barry Bonds' in the majors. The one in Pittsburgh was the unfinished product, still learning, still getting better, but accomplishing quite a bit nonetheless.

"I'm 22 years old and still trying to find out the type of player I am going to be in this game," he said, "the kind of things that are going to make me a successful player."

Everything began coming together for Bonds in 1990. He won his first of a record seven Most Valuable Player awards with a fabulous statistical line as Pittsburgh finished 95-67. Bonds scored 104 runs, hit 33 homers, drove in 114 runs, stole 52 stolen bases and batted that .301.

Bonds had actually lost a salary arbitration case and was not happy about that going into the season, though that was probably the last time anyone in baseball ever said he was not worth the money regardless of the figure. His MVP season proved he was worth whatever he asked for.

"It's a relief," Bonds said, "and I'm gratified. I was only as good as the guys around me. Without the guys in front of me in the lineup, I'm not the MVP."

At times Bonds had been grouchy with sportswriters and believed he would never be able to win a vote from them because he wasn't popular. He had predicted, "They'll screw me. Just watch." That did not happen. One thing that swung voters was that no one else had ever hit .300, stolen 50 bases, driven in 100 runs and scored 100. It was just the beginning of Bonds doing things no one else had ever done in the game.

During the early stages of his career Barry Bonds was often compared to his father, who starring with the Giants was a prototype of a player who could hit 30 homers and steal 30 bases. Barry said he was never as naturally as powerful as father Bobby and had to work to develop the homer power.

"They (baseball people) never got it that my dad was bigger and stronger and didn't have to work at it," Barry Bonds said. "He just walked up to the plate and boom. Me, I have to spend the whole winter in the weight room just to build myself up to play all season."

Bonds accomplished a fair amount with the Pirates, but he became a much big star after leaving Pittsburgh.

Courtesy of the National Baseball Hall of Fame Library

Hall of Famer **Fred Clarke** was probably the most successful player-manager in history. Not only did he bat .312, but he won four pennants with the Pirates.

12
FRED CLARKE

One of the most interesting of Pittsburgh Pirate resumes belongs to Fred Clarke, who not only batted .312 lifetime in a 21-year career, but was also a player-manager in Pittsburgh for 16 years. As the field boss with the Pirates he oversaw the winning of four pennants. Whether such versatility played a part in it or not, Clarke was elected to the Hall of Fame.

Clarke broke into the majors with the Louisville Colonels in 1894, where he stayed until 1900. He became a Pirate after Louisville. He was a 5-foot-10, 165-pound left-fielder who batted left-handed and threw right-handed.

Born in 1872 in Winterset, Iowa, Clarke lived on a farm as a youth as one of 12 children, though the family moved to Kansas when he was two. After playing some semi-pro ball and putting together some solid seasons in the minors, Clarke was grabbed by Louisville. His debut was memorable since he clouted five hits in five trips to the plate, four singles and a triple.

Clarke said he made sure to hang onto the bat that provided such an impressive start.

"When the game was over," he said, "I took the bat into our clubhouse, patted it fondly, and remarked so everybody could hear, 'Well, they had a helluva time knocking this bat out of my hands today.'"

Clarke began playing professionally under unusual circumstances. He spotted a help wanted ad in The Sporting News in 1892 and answered it. He was hired by the Hastings team in the Nebraska State League for $40 a month.

By 1897, when he was just 24, Clarke, who hit .390 that season, was managing the Kentucky club which moved to Pittsburgh at the turn of the 20th century. Clarke played in 2,246 games and accumulated nearly 10,000 at-bats. He batted .300 11 times, six in Pittsburgh. He also collected 509 stolen bases.

Clarke was a good fielder in general, but he had difficulty judging fly balls hit over his head. To compensate Clarke played inordinately deep and took his chances rushing in on the ball. He usually got there, but it made for some adventurous fielding play.

As a man Clarke was greatly admired for fairness and his demeanor. Not only was Clarke considered a good guy, but he did not like to have grumpy players on his team.

"Get results," was Clarke's motto. "A square deal for everybody."

Some other characteristics were identified with Clarke as player and manager. He was known for his hard slides, whether they were taken in attempts to steal bases, or trying to stretch a single into a double. One of his managerial habits, perhaps to ameliorate stress, was chomping on a toothpick when in the dugout. In that he resembled modern-day manager Dusty Baker. Clarke should have had a toothpick manufacturer's endorsement.

However, Clarke gave another reason for why he chewed on a toothpick all of the time. He didn't like talking much and believed if he had something in his mouth he could avoid it.

"I always chew a toothpick to keep from talking," Clarke said once. "The habit keeps my mouth busy, you see. That is the secret, I think, of what little success I have had."

Realistically, though, Clarke had considerable success as a player and a manager. The Pirates appeared in the first World Series in 1903 and he was directing traffic for them. Pittsburgh also won pennants in 1901, 1902 and 1909 with him in charge.

Certainly not someone who seemed boastful about his leadership or playing abilities when it came to assessing his work, Clarke once said, "I attribute my success to fate. Life is a funny game and a little thing, almost a trifle, may make a splash in your affairs so big that the ripples from it will be felt as long as you live."

Once he was cajoled into speaking, apparently Clarke was quite the philosopher.

Such lengthy paragraphs were a rarity in Clarke's personal speaking history. After the Pirates won the World Series in 1909 after a brilliant 110-42 regular-season campaign, Pirates owner Barney Dreyfuss threw a huge banquet as part of the celebration. Of course everyone wanted to hear from the manager, so Clarke was cornered and required to make a speech.

When his turn came Clarke arose and said, "Gentlemen, if I was as poor a manager as I am an orator, the Cubs would be wearing the world's pennant in their park now."

And then Clarke sat down. If his speech could be compared to a ball game he was at the plate for barely one-third of an inning.

One thing about Clarke, though, was that he lived a long life, to age 87, and with many sports reporters giving it a try eventually various nuggets of observation were squeezed out of him.

Clarke, who owned a 1,320-acre ranch in Kansas in retirement, and served in several administrative capacities in non-professional baseball for years, in addition to making money in oil, did offer advice to players who aspired to become major leaguers.

"You've got to love baseball and want to play it above all else," Clarke said. "You have to take every opportunity to practice and play. And not be discouraged. The most important thing is desire."

Clarke, who lived until 1960, called Honus Wagner the best player in history. The reason Clarke gave was, "He had no weakness." Clarke saw Ty Cobb up close and saw many of the superstars of the game, but perhaps he was prejudiced since he managed the man.

Baseball player, manager, league executive, farmer and oil producer, Clarke had a full life. He won 1,422 games as a manager and often was asked how to last in such an ulcer-inducing profession.

“He must learn to smile, smile, smile all the time,” Clarke said, “and smile harder when things go wrong than when they go right. If a team believes the manager is worried and discouraged they are going to be worried and discouraged.”

13
WILBUR COOPER

It goes beyond having a good memory for Pittsburgh Pirates fans to remember Wilbur Cooper. They would need a séance, or a close look at the history books. Cooper is the winningest pitcher in team history with 202 victories while wearing a Pirate uniform. A pretty good achievement since he has been retired since 1926 and has been dead since 1973.

Cooper was a 5-foot-11, 175-pound southpaw from West Virginia who spent most of his career with Pittsburgh—except for the last few inconsequential seasons as his career wound down at 34.

Cooper broke into the majors with the Pirates in 1912. He offered a nice hint of what he might offer in the coming years by going 3-0 with 1.66 earned run average. Cooper remained with the Pirates through the 1924 season—just before Pittsburgh won a pennant. He was traded to the Chicago Cubs before the 1925 season.

Four times Cooper won 20 or more games in a season and two additional times he won 19. Cooper's career high was 23 wins in 1922, but he led the National League with 22 victories in 1921. Overall, Cooper's Major League record was 216-178 with a 2.89 earned run average.

Cooper had some superb ERAs of 1.66, 1.87, and 2.11, but surprisingly, during his seasons with the most wins his ERAs were well over 3.00, a combination that didn't match.

Often called "Coop" as a nickname, Cooper's first name was actually Arley, but he preferred Wilbur.

When Cooper was at his best, he was very good, and there were reports that New York Giants manager John J. McGraw coveted him and offered the Pirates $75,000 for Cooper, but was turned down. Cooper got votes as the best southpaw of his era and he and Grover Cleveland Alexander once engaged in a pitcher's duel that was decided in 59 minutes. Not too many base runners in that one.

"Alexander is the greatest right-handed pitcher I ever saw," Cooper said. "Anybody who can win 30 or more games in that candy box Baker Bowl (in Philadelphia) can walk on the moon."

Cooper was more than an incidental participant in another milestone Pirates game that was played on August 1, 1918. It was Pittsburgh at Boston versus the Braves. Boston's pitcher Art Nehf deserved the lion's share of credit because he pitched 20 innings that day, 20 scoreless innings. Pittsburgh starter Erskine Mayer threw 15 1/3 innings for the Pirates before giving way to Cooper. Cooper pitched five and two-thirds innings to obtain the win when his club scored two runs in the 21st inning. Cooper permitted three hits in his stint.

Cooper actually pitched a shutout in his debut game, an 8-0 triumph over the St. Louis Cardinals. The shutout was preserved by a superb fielding play by shortstop Honus Wagner. Cooper said he called Honus "Mr. Wagner" when he thanked him for the great catch. He said Wagner then praised him and told him to keep getting the opposing batters out. One reason why Cooper recalled the exchange so well, he said, was that he believes that was the first time Wagner spoke to him.

There were times during his prime years when Cooper was either winning 20 games per season or coming close and he inspired a writer in the Pittsburgh Gazette Times named George S. Applegarth to rhapsodize about him in poetry.

In part the poem read in homage to Cooper,

> *"When Wilbur occupies the mound,*
> *That batters famed for biffing,*
> *Are prone to swear and tear their hair,*
> *And beat upon the empty air."*

Tribute aside, Cooper wasn't much of a strikeout pitcher, but as the aces of the time were expected to be, he was a guy who when called upon put in his time on the mound. Twice Cooper threw 327 innings in a season.

Long after he retired Cooper harbored hopes that he might be voted into baseball's Hall of Fame. Such a call never came, though he talked about it occasionally.

"I would die a happy man if they voted me into the Hall of Fame," Cooper said. "But if they don't I will understand. Once people get my age people understand a little more about things than they did when they were younger."

Cooper definitely left a long-term mark on the Pirates. He left the team in 1924 and yet his name pops up on many lists amidst the pitching stats nearly 90 years after he hurled his last pitch for the club. Cooper is first in victories, second in games started with 368, second in innings with 3,201, second in losses with 159, virtually tied for seventh in ERA with a 2.73, first in complete games with 263, fourth in shutouts with 34, and third in strikeouts with 1,194.

If Pirate fans were surprised when Cooper was sent to the Cubs in time for the 1925 season, it did not come close to matching the pitcher's own surprise. He had been the ace of the team and suddenly was shipped out with shortstop Rabbit Maranville and Charlie Grimm for three players who didn't really make much of an impact in Pittsburgh.

"I always regretted never getting into a Series," Cooper said, "but as I look back on my baseball days I guess I did all right by myself."

Cooper's career did slide after the trade, too. He went 12-14 for the Cubs in 1925 and won only four more games total in his career.

In 1959 Cooper was inducted into the Pittsburgh Hall of Fame. Pittsburgh Post-Gazette sports editor Al Abrams was the one who informed Cooper with a telephone call.

"Wait until I grab a chair," Cooper said. "I am flattered, honored and surprised that you would think of me. There are times when old-timers begin to think the younger generation doesn't know a thing about them. I'm happy to know Pittsburgh hasn't forgotten me."

When it comes to the Pittsburgh Pirates it would be impossible to forget Wilbur Cooper given the pitching marks he left behind.

14
SAM LEEVER

One of the greatest pitchers to ever throw for the Pirates Sam Leever ranks third in club history with 193 wins. He spent his entire 13-year Major League career with Pittsburgh, starting in 1898.

Hailing from Goshen, Ohio, the right-handed thrower got a late start in baseball. He grew up on a farm, but was into another profession teaching school over a several-year period. When he ascended to the majors at age 26 he picked up the nickname "The Goshen School Teacher."

The 5-foot-10, 175-pound Leever had many lessons to teach batters, however. While throwing 2,660 2/3 innings in his career, he surrendered just 29 home runs. Leever didn't overpower hitters, rarely striking out more than a handful in a game, but he just didn't give up runs. His lifetime earned run average was 2.47, again third-best in Pirates history.

On his way to a record of 194-100, Leever won at least 20 games for the Pirates four times. In 1899 Leever started 39 games, pitched 379 innings, which led the National League, and posted a 21-23 record, an oddity. In 1900 Leever tossed more than 233 innings and gave up just two home runs.

Leever fared much better in his other 20-victory campaigns. In 1903, a year when the Pirates won the pennant and played in the first World Series, Leever finished 25-7 with a league-leading 2.06 earned run average. Leever got hurt before the Series, though, injuring his right shoulder in a trap shooting contest.

He also finished 20-5 in 1905 and 22-7 in 1906.In 1907, when Leever finished 14-9, his ERA was 1.66. As was common during that era Leever was also a pitcher who finished what he started. In 299 starts Leever pitched 241 complete games. In 1899 he pitched 35 complete games. While primarily a starting pitcher the Pirates also threw Leever into games in relief to try to rescue situations. Three times Leever topped the National League in winning percentage, the best one being the 20-5 season with an .800 mark.

At that time there were no specialist relievers to act as closers and managers simply went with their best pitchers in an emergency if the event came up between starts. An illustration of how Leever was used is the 1899 season when he appeared in 51 games, which led the National League. He led the league in games finished with 11. Whether it was fatigue alone that caused it, or additional circumstances, too, Leever never came close to pitching those 379 innings again.

Leever's heyday coincided with the Pirates winning three straight NL pennants, 1901-1903. The club had spectacular pitching at the time, with Leever, Jack Chesbro, Deacon Phillippe and Jesse Tannehill in the rotation. There was no World Series until 1903 since the National League and American League were feuding.

The Pirates lost the initial Series. Leever pitched with his injury and lost two games, incurring massive press criticism that was controversial. It was even suggested that Leever wasn't trying his best at times. Others came to his defense saying such a hint was scandalous and would be totally out of character for the man they knew. Ralph Davis, a Pittsburgh sports writer, defended Leever in The Sporting News, writing, "The charge that Leever laid down is absurd in the extreme. There is not a more honest man in the game."

Unfortunately for Leever, that Series was the only time he had the opportunity to pitch in the post-season. His final numbers were 0-2 with a 5.40 earned run average.

In 1908 the Pirates felt they had a strong team, but as the season wound down they appeared to be out of contention. Things looked so hopeless that Leever grumpily told his teammates he would sell his World Series share for a dime. Either spying a good investment, or just harboring a never-say-die attitude, Pirate teammates Fred Clarke and Vic Willis each handed him a nickel. The Pirates rallied and came down to the last game of the season needing a victory to tie the Chicago Cubs for the pennant. Pittsburgh lost. While Leever made 10 cents he probably didn't really want, the reaction in reverse if the Pirates had won a pennant and earned a World Series share would likely have caused a considerable hullabaloo if Leever handed his cut over to two teammates.

Leever, however, was part of the Pirates' 1909 championship team. That season, at 37, he finished 8-1 with a 2.83 ERA. But he did not pitch in the Series itself against the Detroit Tigers. Pittsburgh used five other pitchers. It was manager Fred Clarke's choice, made because he felt Leever was slipping since he was giving up more hits, even if he kept escaping without allowing many runs.

It didn't matter so much in the big picture because the Pirates topped the Tigers, anyway, but Clarke may have misjudged Leever. Leever returned for the 1910 season—his last in the big leagues at age 38—finished 6-5 and compiled another first-class ERA of 2.76.

Even after departing the National League Leever retained a taste for pitching, so he joined the Minneapolis Millers in 1911. He won seven games. In 1913 Leever took a position managing a Federal League team, but that concluded his baseball career.

Leever and his wife bought a 70-acre farm in his old home town of Goshen and to whatever degree he raised farm animals or crops, he returned to his first profession, once again becoming "The Goshen School Master."

What seemed to give Leever his greatest pleasure in retirement from the game he loved was going on hunting trips with former teammates such as Honus Wagner and Deacon Phillippe. Leever apparently held no grudge against trap shooting for his ill-timed injury of 1903 because he remained heavily involved in that sport.

Besides being the third-winningest pitcher in Pirates history Leever ranks high on team lists in earned run average, games started, winning percentage (.661), shutouts (39), complete games, and innings pitched.

Courtesy of the National Baseball Hall of Fame Library

For a period of time in the late 1970s **Dave Parker** may have been the best player in baseball. During his stay with the Pirates he won an MVP award, was a four-time All-Star and a three-time Gold Glove winner.

15
DAVE PARKER

His nickname was "The Cobra" and Dave Parker could definitely deliver the kill with one swift strike if you happened to be a Pirates opponent in the way. A mountain of a man at 6-foot-5 and 230 pounds, Parker could clobber the ball.

A left-handed swinger who was born in Mississippi, but who graduated high school in Cincinnati, where he also starred, Parker made his Major League debut with Pittsburgh in 1973 at age 22. It was an OK start, appearing in 54 games with a .288 batting average, but soon enough Parker was making a bigger splash than that.

The right-fielder played most of 11 seasons in Pittsburgh, was a four-time All-Star, a three-time Gold Glove winner, and captured a Most Valuable Player award. He was a two-time National League batting champ.

Parker won his first batting title in 1977 when he hit .338 and also led the NL in hits that year with 215. The next season—Parker's MVP year—was dominating. He batted .334, with 30 home runs, 117 RBIs, 102 runs scored and 20 stolen bases. Every part of his statistical line was fabulous and at 27 really stamped Parker as one of the top players in the league.

In all with the Pirates, Parker batted over .300 five times, drove in more than 100 runs twice, and scored more than 100 three times.

One thing that enhanced Parker's MVP candidacy was his ability to achieve while playing with a broken jaw and cheek bone, necessitating him playing wearing wire face protection. Parker was excited to be named MVP and it only gave him grander goals, though it was difficult to think up many besides team achievement.

"I can win the Triple Crown next year," he said. "I missed a lot of games with my broken cheek bone last summer and I still just missed 200 hits by four and a few other departments I might have won. If I continue swinging freely I'll get my homers and my RBIs. I'll go the other way when they pitch me outside. I don't mind hitting to the opposite field. Sooner or later they're going to have to come inside to me."

Not everything was completely sweetness and light after 1978 because Parker's contract was up and he wanted a lot more money. He asked for $1 million a year for six years or $800,000 a year for 10 years and the Pirates were not a rich franchise.

"I made a mistake the last time I signed," Parker said of agreeing for what he felt was not enough money, "and I don't want to do it again. I would like to stay here in Pittsburgh. Right now I feel I'll be here in Pittsburgh."

Parker was paid $110,000 in 1977, but after his new contract he did reach his $1 million mark—and he did stay in Pittsburgh until after he turned 32 on that five-year pact. It was the sport's first million-dollar contract.

"This is where I want to play," Parker said. "The ball club is my family."

The ball club felt the same about Parker, with manager Chuck Tanner raving about his all-around skills.

"There is no doubt about it," Tanner said, "Dave Parker is the best player in the game today. He is our foundation for the future."

The immediate future was pretty bright. The 1979 season gave Pittsburgh one of its most memorable Pirate teams. The club won the World Series and Parker was a big part of the success. His regular-season numbers were down slightly, but still very strong with 109 runs scored, 25 homers, 94 RBIs and a .310 average. He batted .333 in the National League Championship Series against Cincinnati and .345 in the World Series against Baltimore.

At that point Parker, based on bonuses included, was said to be the highest paid player in the game and he had put together the record to deserve it. His all-around skills shone in the field and at bat and he was in his prime age-wise at 28 during the championship season.

There were some jokes going around at the time, some by Parker, about what he would be worth on the New York Stock Exchange (he also said he had made some good investments).

"But I take more pride in the stock as being known as the best player in the game, or one of the best players in the game," he said. "I get a great deal of satisfaction out of that."

One thing that Parker did not gain satisfaction from is when fans treated him shabbily because of his high-profile, rich contract. At times when they threw things at him on the field Parker was bewildered, especially since he played well the next year and the Pirates won the championship.

"The steel industry was bad and the coal industry was bad and people couldn't relate," Parker said of his big contract. "Their attitudes totally changed toward me. The people hated my very existence, no matter what I did."

He did attribute some of the scorn to his being black.

"If I had been a white guy at the time I had received the money they would have erected a statue to me in that city for all I did," Parker said.

Parker, who played 19 seasons with a .290 average, spent several productive years with his hometown Cincinnati Reds, but in 1985 was caught up in the legal system when several ex-Pirates were implicated in cocaine trials. They testified under immunity, but some players were suspended for a year by Major League Baseball. However, their sentences were modified based on the proviso that they donate 10 percent of salaries to drug awareness programs, perform community service, and undergo drug testing. Parker was one of those players and his involvement tarnished his legacy.

After retiring in 1991 Parker did work as a coach for some big-league clubs. His time on the regular Hall of Fame ballot expired without his selection.

16
GINGER BEAUMONT

The red-head from Rochester, Wisconsin did some extraordinary things on the diamond after breaking into the big leagues in 1899, especially since his career lasted just 12 years and he was retired by age 33. Most of that Major League service time accrued with the Pirates over eight seasons ending in 1906.

Beaumont represented Pittsburgh well. He batted over .300 six times, including in 1902 when he won the National League batting title with a .357 average. Beaumont, Pittsburgh's everyday center fielder, also led the NL in hits four times, three of those times with Pittsburgh, scored at least 100 runs for the Pirates four times while leading the league in 1903 with 137, and stole about 30 bases a year.

On a smaller scale, but equally impressive, Beaumont notched some other notable achievements. In a game his rookie year Beaumont managed six infield singles.

"On my fourth try, the third baseman stood 10 feet from the plate and I still beat out a bunt," Beaumont said.

He also became the first player to score six runs in a game. In 1903, when the Pirates participated in the first World Series against the Boston Red Sox the opening game was in the home of the American League team, so Pittsburgh batted first. As the Pirates' leadoff hitter, that meant that Beaumont became the first player to bat in a World Series.

Born in 1876, Beaumont, whose given name was Clarence Howeth Beaumont and picked up the nickname because of his hair color, attended Beloit College in Wisconsin before turning to baseball.

The 1903 Series capped Pittsburgh's run of three straight National League pennants and it marked the first inter-league championship bout with the American League, hence the grand name of World Series. Game 1 was played at the Huntington Avenue Grounds (pre-Fenway Park) on October 1, 1903 and that brought Beaumont to the plate first. The opposing pitcher for Boston was Cy Young. Young won the match-up, with Beaumont flying to center field.

Beaumont stood 5-foot-8 and weighed 190 pounds. In the deadball era he was not much of a home-run threat, never collecting more than eight in a year and accumulating just 39 altogether in his career. He slashed line drives. That was his trademark. Beaumont duped many pitchers with his demeanor. He invoked a lazy-looking style when he stepped into the batter's box, but when he coiled and unleashed his swing the ball traveled.

On other occasions Beaumont exploded out of the batter's box on bunts or infield hits. He dashed down the first-base line with considerable speed and often created hits out of balls hit 90 feet or less.

Beaumont batted .352 as a rookie, dropped off the next season, and then regained his stroke. He then in order batted .332, .357, .341, .301, and .328. Beaumont both manufactured hits and clouted worthy hits.

One of Beaumont's biggest fans was Pirate all-timer Honus Wagner, a teammate in the early 20th century. Wagner, who stuck around the game much longer as a coach, once selected an all-time team and he put Beaumont on the roster of this imaginary aggregation. Wagner very much appreciated Beaumont's hitting style and success and said he would have thrived in the lively ball era.

"Ginger made 200 hits with the ball that was a chunk of mud compared to the modern rabbit," Wagner said. "If he could have hit the golf ball they use today he would have made (Babe) Ruth, (Goose) Goslin and (Al) Simmons look bad."

In 1906, Beaumont's hitting tailed off to a .265 average. Pittsburgh rather quickly gave up on him, trading him to the Boston Beaneaters along with Patsy Flaherty and Claude Ritchey for infielder Ed

Abbaticchio. Abbaticchio played two full seasons and small parts of two others for Pittsburgh, but never was more than a middling mid-.200s hitter. Flaherty twice won 12 games for Boston and Ritchey started in the outfield for a couple of seasons.

Beaumont was unhappy to be shipped out of Pittsburgh, but his first season for the team that would become the Braves he batted .322 and led the NL in hits. After that Beaumont's career tapered off.

Beaumont's baseball tenure was cut short by injury. In the early part of the 1900s an athlete who suffered a serious knee injury, a torn anterior cruciate or the like, was practically finished. Medical science was flummoxed by the knee at that juncture in history and could offer no repair suggestion beyond rest and strengthening. Beaumont's legs began bothering him and a knee problem flared up reducing his effectiveness even more.

In 1910 Beaumont was moved to the Chicago Cubs, but in a good break the Cubs became pennant winners that year and he got another World Series shot. By that year Beaumont was no longer operating on all cylinders. He got into 76 games and batted .267, mostly as a fourth outfielder and pinch-hitter, though his on-base percentage was .373.

The Cubs faced the Philadelphia Athletics in the Series. Both teams had been superb during the regular season. The A's won the American League pennant with a mark of 102-48 and the Cubs ruled the National League with a mark of 104-50. Beaumont lucked into something good for his final year in the majors.

Philadelphia won the Series and Beaumont did not play in the field, only being used on three occasions as a pinch-hitter. He walked once and scored a run, but did not hit safely. The Cubs released him after the season.

Beaumont played a final year of minor league ball in St. Paul, Minnesota in 1911, and then retired to a 180-acre farm in Honey Creek, Wisconsin. Selected for the Wisconsin Athletic Hall of Fame, Beaumont also has a Little League named after him in that state. He served as a public official, a county supervisor near his home, but two strokes contributed to first his being limited in a wheelchair, and then to his death, at 79, in a Wisconsin hospital.

Courtesy of the National Baseball Hall of Fame Library

When the Pirates were winning three straight pennants in the early 1900s **Deacon Phillippe** was one of their biggest winners. He pitched five complete games in the 1903 World Series, going 3-2.

17
DEACON PHILLIPPE

A late comer to the majors, Charles Louis Phillippe earned his stripes as well as his nickname Deacon from pitching superbly from his rookie year on. He made his debut at age 27 for the Louisville Colonels in 1899, but spent the rest of his 13-year career with the Pirates.

The link between the expiration of Louisville and the Pittsburgh club was a strong one. When Louisville was going belly up Pirates owner Barney Dreyfuss swooped in and signed every good player he could from Louisville and employed them with the Pirates. Phillippe was one of them.

Phillippe had gone 21-17 for Louisville as a rookie with a 3.17 earned run average. One way he got people's attention was by pitching a no-hitter in his seventh start. The victory was hurled over the New York Giants on May 25, 1899 and the Colonels won 7-0.

Although Phillippe was already 28 by the time he joined the Pirates for the 1900 season he showed improvement, finishing 20-13 with a 2.84 earned run average. Between Phillippe's inaugural season and his first four years with the Pirates he won at least 20 games in five straight years. He added a sixth overall 20-game season and a fifth with the Pirates in 1905.

A sturdy right-hander, Phillippe was 6 feet tall and weighed 180 pounds. In some ways Phillippe, who always maintained a quiet demeanor, was fortunate to have found his way to pro ball at all. He was born in tiny Rural Retreat, Virginia, with the name of the place saying it all about its smallness. It was too small for Phillippe's family apparently because the clan moved to South Dakota when he was a boy. It wasn't until 1897 that Phillippe broke into the minors and swiftly gained sufficient acclaim to be sought by the big leagues.

Phillippe won 21, 20, 22, 20 and 25 games in a row at the beginning of his career. The showcase 25-9 season was posted in 1903, the year the Pirates competed in the first World Series. The opponent was the Boston Americans, or Red Sox, and while the AL club captured the title Phillippe distinguished himself for all time.

That was the year Pittsburgh's other ace, Sam Leever, was at less than full strength for the October match-up, which shifted the load of expectations to Phillippe. Cy Young, the winningest pitcher of all time, was the Boston starter in the first game and Phillippe drew the nod from Pirates manager Fred Clarke.

While it has often been noted that the famous Young, who later had the Cy Young Award named after him to honor his prowess, appeared in that contest, it is not as well-recalled that Phillippe actually won the game, 7-3. Pittsburgh scored four runs in the first inning. That was only the beginning of the responsibilities shouldered by Phillippe.

"I felt I could have beaten any team I ever faced that afternoon," Phillippe said.

The first game was played on October 1 and at first Boston and Pittsburgh played every day without a break. The first three games were at Boston's Huntington Avenue Grounds with no days off in-between. Phillippe returned to the mound for Game 3 on October 3 and won again, this time 4-2. Boston was allowed just four hits.

Phillippe's timing was impeccable. There was now a break in the Series until October 6, giving Phillippe plenty of rest for Game 4 which was played at Exposition Park in Pittsburgh. That was the forerunner to the team's Forbes Field home. Phillippe finished his third straight complete-game win, 5-4, although he faltered in the ninth inning, nearly allowing Boston to bounce back from a 5-1 deficit.

This was not a best-four-out of-seven Series, but five-out-of-nine. Phillippe next pitched in Game 7 against Cy Young and the Cyclone topped the Deacon, 7-3. By now it was quite possible that Phillippe was suffering some arm fatigue. But Clarke kept running him out to the mound. Game 8 was scheduled for October 13 and Phillippe was the assigned Pittsburgh pitcher for the fifth time in the Series. Boston relied on Bill Dineen for the fourth time.

What began as a scoreless tie was disrupted by two Boston runs off Phillippe in the fourth inning with the Red Sox pulling away for a 3-0 win. The Pirates managed just four hits. Pitching five complete World Series games between October 1 and 13 were viewed as a somewhat heroic effort by Phillippe.

Phillippe may have been a quiet individual, but he was a steely competitor. He relished facing the other teams' best pitchers when their turns in the rotation came around.

"In my time there was no such thing as 'spot' pitchers," Phillippe said, "hurlers who were thrown against certain teams because they could lick 'em. We went against everybody and the slogan was 'The bigger and tougher they are, the harder they fall.' Take, for instance, when Mordecai Brown and Christy Mathewson used to come to town. We'd all ask to tangle with the star of the other mound staff. We'd even beg to pitch against Brown or Matty, or any of the tough guys."

For other teams' pitchers, Phillippe was one of the tough guys. His career record was 189-109 and he won 167 games for the Pirates, fifth on the team's all-time list. His earned run average of 2.51 is fourth in the club record book.

In 1906 and 1907 when Phillippe was entering his mid-30s his work load declined, but he still won 15 and 14 games, respectively, for the Pirates with sub-3.00 earned run averages. In 1910, Phillippe produced one additional gem of a season, finishing 14-2 with a 2.29 ERA at age 38.

Later in life, after leaving baseball, Phillippe worked in a steel mill and then started a fresh career as bailiff in a county court. One of his descendants is the popular actor Ryan Phillippe who in 2003 named his son Deacon after the pitcher who died in 1952.

Courtesy of the National Baseball Hall of Fame Library

In 1960 shortstop **Dick Groat** won the National League batting title with a .325 mark and was rewarded with the Most Valuable Player award as the Pirates won the championship.

18
DICK GROAT

The magic year during Dick Groat's long stay with the Pittsburgh Pirates was 1960. That was probably the most magical year in the history of the franchise, the year when the underdog Pirates won the World Series in seven games over the New York Yankees.

That season the animated shortstop batted .325 to win the National League batting title, was chosen for the All-Star team, and won the NL Most Valuable Player award. That was the signature season of Groat's nine-year stay with the Pirates, a stint that began in 1952 and was interrupted for two years by military service.

In 1960 Groat was a leader on a team of leaders, the top hitter for average on a team of clutch hitters. He was a holler guy in the field and it was the capstone of his Pittsburgh stay.

Born in Wilkinsburg, Pennsylvania in 1930, Groat graduated from high school in Swissvale, Pennsylvania and retired to the suburbs of Pittsburgh. In-between, his baseball career took him elsewhere, notably to the St. Louis Cardinals for some critical years, but he is best-recalled as a Pirate.

Groat was 5-foot-11 and 180 pounds and a tremendous all-around athlete. He attended Duke University where he was a basketball star—the storied Blue Devils' program's first All-American. He led the NCAA in scoring and played a year for the Fort Wayne Pistons in the NBA before committing fully to baseball.

The heady shortstop first signed with the Pirates in the summer of 1952 after completing his college basketball career. The famed administrator Branch Rickey came to his home to proffer a deal to

Groat that was estimated to include a $50,000 bonus. The contract was a big deal and received media coverage given Groat's background. Rickey and young, short-haired Groat were photographed shaking hands with Groat's father Martin overlooking the scene.

Despite that mini-ceremony, the official announcement was made at Forbes Field and Groat was gung-ho to begin his baseball career. He had grown up a Pirates fan and now he was one.

"This is something I've always wanted to do," he said, "become a Pittsburgh Pirate."

He became one that summer and played in 95 games, batting .284 as a rookie. Groat certainly demonstrated potential quickly. In one 1952 game he smacked five singles in a game against the Boston Braves. Groat got some attention on his first visit to New York City soon after the signing, partially because he had recently played basketball for Duke at Madison Square Garden and was remembered for that.

"I believe I can field in the majors," Groat said, "and I certainly hope I can hit in the majors."

Although it seemed likely that the right-handed hitter would have been a key cog in the team the next season, Groat disappeared off the roster for two years doing military time. He did not play for the Pirates again until 1955 when he became a full-time regular and batted .267.

Once he eased into his role Groat began to make his mark. He hit .315 in 1957 and .300 in 1958. Groat was becoming one of the most important players on the team as a Pirates club that had been horrible in the early 1950s gradually improved and began moving up in the standings. By then manager Danny Murtaugh was calling Groat "the indispensable Pirate."

After a couple of years in the big leagues putting up good averages, Groat had learned he could hit top-level pitching.

"I always had confidence in my hitting," Groat said somewhat in contrast to what he uttered when he first signed, “because I don’t strike out much. And as long as you get a piece of the ball a batter does all right.”

Besides being an excellent player, besides being a key leader on a team that needed leadership—he became captain--Groat came off in public as modest and self-assuming, and, as one sportswriter said, as someone who didn’t believe the nice things people said about him.

Pirates’ general manager Joe Brown sounded as if he was ready to adopt Groat, never mind pay him to play ball.

“If my 11-year-old son grows up to be the man Groat is he’d make me very happy,” Brown said.

In 1958 Groat was presented with the Dapper Dan Award as the top sports figure of the year in the Pittsburgh area. He received the honor at a dinner in front of 1,200 people.

“This is the thrill of a lifetime,” Groat said, though he may have amended that comment two years later. “I’m accepting this award as a responsibility for my three ideals in the way of sports and the way of life: Dedication, performance and humility.”

The Pirates big push came in 1960. There was alarm when in the beginning of September Groat was hit by a pitch thrown by Milwaukee’s Lew Burdette. Groat tried to block the inside throw with his left hand and the ball broke his wrist.

Burdette apologized to Groat, saying, “I’m awfully sorry, Dick. It was a slider and it just got away from me.”

Groat missed 14 games and there was some question whether he would be able to play in the Series after being stuck in a cast. It wasn’t going to be easy to keep Groat out of the Series and he did play. Groat came to bat 28 times in the seven games and batted .214 with two RBIs and three runs scored.

After the Pirates became champs the regular-season MVP was announced. Groat won the vote, but there were four Pirates among the top eight NL vote-getters.

"This is a tremendous thrill and honor every player dreams of, but so few win," Groat said. "It happens once in a lifetime."

Groat later starred for the St. Louis Cardinals, another World Series winner. In retirement he and former teammate Jerry Lynch opened the Champions Lake Golf Club in Ligonier, Pennsylvania and since 1979 Groat worked as a radio color commentator for the University of Pittsburgh men's basketball team.

19
JESSE TANNEHILL

Given that Jesse Tannehill broke into the majors in 1894, he is probably not a household name in too many households in the greater Pittsburgh area. Although he excelled for the Pirates the fans of long ago also likely wished he had stayed around longer than he did.

Of all of the pitchers who have pitched for the Pirates since the founding of the franchise Tannehill has the best winning percentage of any who posted 100 decisions. Just during his time with Pittsburgh Tannehill compiled a 116-58 record for a .667 winning percentage.

Tannehill had a 15-year Major League career and six of those seasons were spent in Pittsburgh. During that time he was as much a fixture on the mound as the three rivers were as geographical features. In those years Tannehill won as many as 25 games and only once dipped below 18 wins.

Born in Dayton, Kentucky in 1874, Jesse Niles Tannehill spent most of his life residing in that area. His home away from home was the pitcher's mound and besides Pittsburgh he also played for the Cincinnati Reds and for such American League teams as Boston and Washington. Tannehill recorded four 20-win seasons for the Pirates and two more for the Red Sox.

Given that he was just 5-foot-8 and weighed 150 pounds it was somewhat remarkable that Tannehill had the stuff to get hitters out with such frequency. A tricky curve ball was credited. Tannehill's lifetime earned run average was 2.80, but his primo seasonal ERA was 1.95 with the Pirates in 1902. He also led the National League in earned run average in 1901 with a 2.18 mark.

Tannehill's overall record was 197-117 and as was the hallmark of pitchers during the deadball era when he took the ball from the manager and he planned to go nine every time out. Tannehill had seasons for Pittsburgh when he threw 34 and 33 complete games.

In 1898, Tannehill tossed 326 2/3 innings for Pittsburgh and the next year he hurled 322 innings.

Tannehill was first spotted as a big-league prospect by the Cincinnati Reds and had a cameo in the National League in 1894 at 19. He went 1-1 with a 7.14 earned run average and it was suggested that he needed more seasoning. His next appearance in the majors was for the Pirates in 1897. By then he was 22, but he didn't knock management's socks off yet. He did show enough to stick with the team with his 9-9 record and a 4.25 ERA.

Everything changed for Tannehill in 1898, the next season. He had matured, knew his stuff as a pitcher, and immediately emerged as one of the top flingers in the NL. Tannehill became a somebody in a hurry, putting up a 25-13 record with a 2.95 ERA. Tannehill was no strikeout artist, but teams did not score many runs off of him.

Showing that 1898 was no fluke, Tannehill finished 24-14 the next year with a 2.82 earned run average. In 1899 he did it all over again, going 20-6 with a 2.88 earned run average. It was curious, the quirks of the game, that the next season, 1900, when Tannehill recorded league-leading ERA he finished just 18-10. In 1901, though, Tannehill's record of 20-6 was commensurate with his career best 1.95 ERA.

Tannehill was only 27 during the 1902 season. He was one of the dominating pitchers on the Pirates' great staff that had already procured pennants in 1901 and 1902 and it seemed likely there would be a long marriage between the hurler and the team.

However, Major League baseball was in upheaval at the time. The American League had come into being and Tannehill and his pal Jack Chesbro (also a top Pirates pitcher who lifetime went 70-38 with the Bucs) thought they could fetch more money in the new league. They jumped to the New York Highlanders, which later changed their name to the Yankees, for the 1903 season.

By doing so Tannehill missed out on being part of a third straight National League pennant champion and playing in the first World Series. Meanwhile, he did not fare especially well in New York, bringing home a 15-15 record with a 3.27 ERA.

Tannehill's flirtation with the Big Apple lasted just one year and he moved on to Boston, where he did much better, winning 22 and 21 games his first two seasons, and 13 in his last full year in the majors. On August 17, 1904, Tannehill pitched a no-hitter against the Chicago White Sox. Tannehill's brother Lee was also a major leaguer and was in the line-up for Chicago that day at third base and went 0-for-3. Although he managed to spend 10 years in the majors, all with the White Sox, Lee Tannehill was a lifetime .220 hitter.

"I didn't know I had a no-hitter going until the eighth inning," Jesse Tannehill said. "Then a player told me. That's when I began to get nervous. You're even more nervous after the game when you have time to reflect."

Tannehill fizzled out rather quickly after 1907 and ironically concluded his big-league career almost exactly as he began it. Tannehill pitched one game for the Reds and went 0-0 in 1911.

Although his prowess was tangential to his pitching skill, Tannehill was a solid hitter for a pitcher and sometimes his teams employed him in the outfield. He came to bat between 100-and-something and 250 times in a year and finished with a .255 lifetime batting average. Tannehill's finest swatting occurred during the 1900 season when he batted .336 for the Pirates in 120 plate appearances.

Jesse Tannehill disappeared from the majors after his one-shot showing with Cincinnati in 1911, but he did not disappear from baseball. He continued to play in the minors for a couple of additional years and later managed in the minors in Virginia and Topeka, Kansas, and then became a minor-league umpire for a handful of years. He died at 82 in 1956.

Courtesy of the National Baseball Hall of Fame Library

Vic Willis burnished his reputation during his stay with the Pirates sufficiently to become a Hall of Fame hurler. Four years in a row he won more than 20 games for Pittsburgh.

20
VIC WILLIS

His time in Pittsburgh was almost too short for Vic Willis to be considered a special historical figure for the Pirates, but his record is too overwhelming to ignore. The Pirates count him in their record book as the pitcher owning the best earned run average of all time.

Willis played just four seasons for the Pirates, the minimum really, to be viewed as enough of a Pirate to be one of their greats. But what seasons they were. The 6-foot-2, 200-pound right-hander spent 1906, 1907, 1908 and 1909 in a Bucs uniform after spending the largest chunk of his 13-year Major League career with the Boston Beaneaters.

A future Hall of Famer, Willis' records with the Pirates read this way: 1906, 23-13, 1.73 earned run average; 1907, 21-11, 2.34 ERA; 1908, 23-11, 2.07 ERA; and 1909, 22-11, 2.24 ERA. All told that made Willis' won-loss record while in the employ of the Pirates 89-46 with a 2.08 ERA.

That was a winning percentage of .659 and really is what put Willis into the Hall of Fame. While he had some great seasons in Boston, four of them 20-win campaigns and with as many 27 victories in a season, he also had some losing records and his overall percentage wasn't close to what he achieved with the Pirates.

It was almost miraculous in a negative way some of the seasons that Willis ended up with while pitching for Boston. In 1904 he was 18-25 and the next year he was 12-29. The 18 wins came in a season when Boston won just 55 games. The 29 defeats are the most in a single season by a pitcher since 1900. During a three-year period Willis' Braves simply did not score runs and although he had an ERA of 3.02 during that stretch he lost 72 games. No doubt Willis' December 1905 trade to Pittsburgh came as a relief to him. The Pirates gave up three players, none of whom accomplished much, although pitcher Vive Lindaman won 12, 11, and 12 games for Boston over the next three years. Acquiring Willis at that price was one of the greatest trades in Pirates history.

Twice before that when the National League and fledgling American League were feuding Willis was offered good paydays by both the Philadelphia Athletics and Detroit Tigers and nearly jumped both times. In the end he remained with Boston, presumably because the Beaneaters either matched, or came close to matching the salaries offered.

Lifetime, Willis was 249-205 with a 2.63 earned run average. His stay with the Pirates won over Veterans Committee voters in 1995, long after he passed away. During one of those good early seasons with Boston Willis tossed a recognized no-hitter. On August 7, 1899 he bested Washington, 7-1. Further research of accounts of the time suggest that a play called E-6 could have been a single, however.

Since he had suffered through those losing seasons with Boston, sportswriters suggested that Willis was finished. However, when Pittsburgh made the deal Willis actually wrote to Pirates owner Barney Dreyfuss to reassure him that he was not getting damaged goods.

"Don't believe those tales you hear of me being all-in," Willis said. "Wait until you see me in action for your team and then form your opinion of my worth. I assure you that I am delighted to be a Pirate and that I will do my best to bring another pennant to the Smokey City."

Victor Gazaway Willis was born in Maryland in 1876, but his family moved to Newark, Delaware when he was young. Willis attended the University of Delaware and made his Major League debut with the franchise that was later known as the Braves in 1898 when he was 22. His rookie year Willis finished 25-13. His next season he finished 27-8 and led the National League with a 2.50 earned run average. Including his stay in Boston and his time in Pittsburgh Willis recorded eight 20-victory seasons.

As a connection to his college days Willis was called "The Delaware Peach" by some. Willis tossed 50 shutouts in the big leagues and he pitched just shy of 4,000 innings, including an astonishing 410 in 1902. Mr. Workhorse topped 300 innings seven other times, including twice in Pittsburgh. He also threw 388 complete games out of his 471 starts.

Willis did help the Pirates reach the World Series of 1909, his only appearance in the October Classic. At one point during the season Willis won 11 games in a row. He appeared in two games in the Series against the Detroit Tigers with a 0-1 record. However, the Pirates won the title, the only championship of Willis' Major League career.

After the 1909 season the Pirates let Willis go—that despite his 22-11 record. He hooked on with the St. Louis Cardinals at 34 and was felt to have some good years left. It did not turn out that way. Willis went 9-12 and then retired.

Once he got out of baseball Willis returned to Newark, Delaware. He pitched some semi-pro ball, but his big move was buying the Washington Hotel in that town and he became the proprietor/operator. It wasn't very easy for Willis to save up cash from his ball playing days in order to purchase his dream property, either.

At one point Willis talked of the hard negotiating he endured to obtain a $2,400 salary from Boston after his 27-8 year when he led the NL in seven categories.

"I got the $2,400," Willis said, "but a player pretty much had to be a star to get that much dough in those days." The team philosophy at the time was not to simply rest rotation pitchers for a few days, but to keep them busy, he added. "...a pitcher was called on every other afternoon or so, just to keep them from going stale or loafing."

Willis died of a stroke in 1947, nearly a half century before he was chosen for the Hall of Fame.

> “***You have to have your team score some runs for you.***”
>
> – Roy Face

21
ROY FACE

It is so terribly difficult to truly measure Roy Face's career because he was a relief pitcher when they weren't valued so highly, pitched late in games when there was no such thing as a "closer," and didn't win enough games for the Pirates to make the team's all-time top-10 list.

Yet there is no denying his contributions to the Pirates were special. Not only did Face appear in a team record 802 games as a pitcher, he recorded one of the best single seasons of any pitcher in baseball history when he finished 18-1 in 1959.

Face spent 16 years in the majors, all but the last few with Pittsburgh. His career record was 104-95 and he accumulated 193 saves, three times leading the National League in that category. The kind of work Face did for the Pirates in the 1950s and 1960s is the kind that is prized much more highly in importance in the 2000s than it was then. He also handled far more innings in relief than is common in the modern era when pitchers may only appear for an inning or less at a time.

In size Face more resembled the Pirates' star pitchers of the late 1800s or early 1900s. He was 5-foot-8 and weighed 155 pounds. It helped that he did not have to rely on a fastball to get batters out, but had a forkball which was pretty much his alone for success over the years.

"He may be just 5-8, but when he comes marching out of that bullpen to the mound, I'll bet he looks 8-5 to the batters," said Pirates manager Danny Murtaugh.

Elroy Leon Face was born in Stephentown, New York in 1928, but still lives in the Pittsburgh area where he is well-remembered and appreciated for his contributions to the Pirates as they rebuilt in the

1950s and captured the 1960 World Series. He has remained active in Pittsburgh Pirate charities, especially golf tournaments, and has been known for his willingness to sign autographs for fans. Face was already 25 when he broke in with the Pirates in 1953 and went 6-8 as a rookie.

That was an inauspicious start for someone who did not reappear in the majors until 1955, but who also became a six-time All-Star (this was during the period when there were two All-Star games each season and Face was chosen for both three times). Face first displayed signs of the durability that would be the hallmark of his career in 1956 when he broke the team record for most appearances in a season with 68. That led the National League. Face equaled that mark in 1960, also leading the league.

Face's relief pitching really began taking off during the 1958 season and continued all of the way through the 1959 campaign when he recorded one of the most amazing seasons of all time. Face had a five-game winning streak going when 1958 ended and won his first 17 games of the 1959 season. Face went a month at a time without giving up a run.

The hurler finished 1958 with a 2.89 earned run average and 1959 with a 2.70 ERA. Three times Face led the National League in saves with marks of 20, 17, and 28. He collected 24 saves during the World Series year and won 10 games, but he did not lead the NL in saves that season.

As an illustration of how things were done during Face's era Pirates players had to find their own parking spaces when they came to Forbes Field to play, but when he got off to a hot start at the beginning of the 1959 season the attendant at the Esso Station where he regularly left his car waved the $1 fee and said he wouldn't have to pay until he lost a game.

"Turns out, I didn't have to pay until September," Face said, seeming tickled by the situation.

Face's winning percentage was .947 that year, the best ever by any pitcher with at least 15 decisions in a season. Not only was the $1 parking fee inexpensive by current standards, but player salaries were, too. Many years later, Hank Foiles, one of Face's catchers who marveled at his 22-0 two-season streak remarked about the difference.

"If he had that kind of season today," Foiles said in 2009, "you'd need a Brinks truck to pay him."

Face's out pitch was a forkball, but is akin to the split-fingered fastball used now and when asked what the difference is Face joked, "About $3 million a year."

It wasn't as if Face was perfect in every game that 18-1 season because he had some good luck. When he gave up runs the Pirates made a comeback to give him the triumph.

"I could have lost three or four games that year, but we'd get some runs in the bottom of the ninth and I'd get the win," Face said. "You have to have your team score some runs for you."

The Pirates scored all the runs they needed in 1960 to capture the pennant and best the Yankees in the World Series. Murtaugh labeled Face "Sam Spade" for his ability to solve the club's problems. He performed that very duty during the seven-game Series, picking up saves in three out of the four Pirate triumphs.

"Winning was the greatest feeling I ever had in baseball," Face said of claiming that championship, "especially against a team like the Yankees. Through my career the Yankees were the big team."

For years after he left baseball Face worked as a carpenter. He had obtained a union card and hung on to it.

"I always kept my carpenter's union card up to date when I was pitching," Face said. "I worked a little during the winters. I knew I would need it some day."

Face also spent much of his post-pitching career using his free time to fish on a favorite lake where he had established a getaway place years earlier.

> ***I don't really look at myself as a power hitter.***
>
> – Andrew McCutchen

22
ANDREW McCUTCHEN

The speedy center fielder is the cornerstone of the current Pittsburgh Pirates team that is experiencing a resurgence after missing the National League playoffs for more than two decades. His career is too fresh for him to be listed as a more important Pirate on an all-time list today, but all indications are that he will continue to improve and accomplish more.

McCutchen was just 26 during the 2013 season when he led the Pirates out of the gloom of sub-.500 records to a 94-game winning season and into the playoffs for the first time since 1992.

The 5-foot-10, 190-pound star is originally from Fort Meade, Florida and 2013 was just his fifth season in the majors. Thus far McCutchen has been chosen for three All-Star teams and has won a Gold Glove.

An all-around player with speed, power and a good eye at the plate, McCutchen batted .317 in 2013 after batting .327 in 2012. That raised his lifetime average to .296 with an on-base percentage of .380. McCutchen led the NL with 194 hits in 2012. During his five seasons McCutchen has averaged exactly 20 stolen bases a year and almost exactly 20 home runs per season. His high for steals was 33 in 2010 and his high for homers was 31 in 2012.

McCutchen, who plays with his dark hair tied behind him in dreadlocks, was destined for stardom young. He played—and excelled—on his high school team as an eighth grader and ran on a state champion relay team in track. He intended to attend the University of Florida, but when the Pirates drafted him in 2005 he chose professional baseball.

By 2006 McCutchen was already touted as the Pittsburgh organization's minor league player of the year. As a rookie he hit 12 home runs with 54 RBIs, 22 stolen bases and a .286 average in 108 games. Included was one stunning game on August 1 against the Washington Nationals. McCutchen hit three home runs, a solo shot, a two-run homer and a three-run homer. It was a six-RBI day.

During the 2010 season McCutchen produced a five-hit day against the Chicago Cubs and scored five runs, too. All fives. It was like a slot machine paying off in Las Vegas. Actually, McCutchen only stole two bases. One of the hits was a home run.

Teammate Garrett Jones admired the day of work McCutchen put in from the spot right behind him in the batting order.

"The home run he hit went out in about a second," Jones said. "Those lasers he was hitting, he had a great bunt today, so he did it all. It was fun to hit behind him, that's for sure."

Rather remarkably, Jones had five hits in the same game.

McCutchen made it obvious he wasn't going anywhere but PNC Park in a Pirates uniform for quite some time, either. He signed a six-year, $51.5 million deal that carries him through the 2017 season.

During the 2011 season McCutchen joined the Pirates' 20-20 club, with at least 20 home runs and 20 steals in the same year, an example of the type of versatility McCutchen provides.

"It's a special feat," said Pirates manager Clint Hurdle. "It's a special feat in any era. It speaks to the skill set."

It is difficult to really pinpoint McCutchen's coming out, but his career can be drawn with an arrow pointing up on a chart each year. It's definitely been steady improvement.

"His strike-zone discipline this year has been really good," said Pirates general manager Neal Huntington in 2011. "He has as quick hands as anyone in baseball. He generates explosiveness off the bat. He is maturing before our eyes, and it's really fun to see."

Hurdle is a daily eyewitness to McCutchen's development and he is a fan of what he has seen over the last couple of years.

"He's just scratching the surface for me," Hurdle said. "He expects a lot from himself. McCutchen truly wants to play on a championship ball club and he wants to do what he can to help that happen."

Despite making his contributions with long ball swats periodically McCutchen doesn't count himself amongst the game's home-run hitters. He sees his home runs coming as a byproduct of the way he takes his cuts.

"I don't really look at myself as a power hitter," McCutchen said. "I look at myself as someone who drives the balls to the gaps, hits line drives."

McCutchen emerged as the type of player who can carry a team in 2012, but better for him in 2013 he had help all around him in the batting order. While he played just as well the added firepower was the difference maker in turning the once-ragged Pirates of the early 2000s into a playoff team. Not that it was believed the club would fare well without him if McCutchen should be injured and with just a couple of days left in the regular season the player and the franchise got a scare. While distracted McCutchen was hit in the head by a fly ball during practice.

In tune with the modern social media options, McCutchen wasted no time in letting the Pirates fan base know he was OK by humorous tweeting. He wrote, "The ball that hit me will be out for the remainder of the postseason with 5 ripped seams and a bruised ego." The good news was that McCutchen was intact.

Under the revamped Major League playoff structure starting in 2012 each league advanced two non-division winners, or wild-card choices, into the playoffs. Pittsburgh was runner-up to the St. Louis Cardinals in the National League Central Division, but it so happened that the next best team was the Cincinnati Reds, the team that finished right behind the Pirates in the regular-season standings.

Pittsburgh hosted its first playoff game in more than 20 years and trounced the Reds, 6-2 to advance.

"We're for real," McCutchen said. "We're definitely for real."

23
BOB FRIEND

The right-hander from Lafayette, Indiana was a fixture on the Pirates pitching staff from 1951 to 1966, playing all 16 of his Major League seasons in Pittsburgh except for his last year, and then settling in the area after retirement.

Friend won 191 games for the Pirates, fourth-most in team history, and was a member of the 1960 World Series champions. Friend was a three-time All-Star who also endured the aggravation of playing on some of the worst Pittsburgh teams ever and paid the price with a large number of losses on his record.

Born in 1930, Friend grew up in Indiana and attended Purdue University. The 6-foot, 190-pound thrower was just 20 when he made his big-league debut as the Pirates sought to rebuild the club from the ashes up. Friend went right into the rotation as a rookie and finished 6-10 during his first season.

Friend pretty much learned on the job for the weak-hitting Pirates over his first four seasons, digging himself a sub-.500 mark of 28-50 before turning things around. When Friend did so, it was in a big way during the 1955 season. That year he finished 14-9 and led the National League with a 2.83 earned run average. The most notable aspect of Friend's ERA achievement was that he became the first pitcher to lead a league in earned run average while playing for a last-place team. Pittsburgh finished 38 ½ games out of first place.

That was the first of nine double-figure victory seasons for Friend with the Pirates. Five times he won at least 17 games and in 1958 he led the NL in wins with 22. Twice, including 1956, Friend pitched the most innings in the league, that season hitting 314 1/3.

A steady innings consumer, Friend led the NL in games started three times.

In the memorable 1960 Series title-winning year, Friend went 18-12 with a 3.00 earned run average and made the All-Star team.

Growing up Friend played football, basketball, baseball and golf and it was his aspiration to play football for the Purdue Boilermakers where several relatives had attended school. However, an injury made Friend concentrate his athletic endeavors on baseball. He struck out 21 out of 22 batters in one high school game.

General manager Branch Rickey was desperately seeking to reverse the abysmal fortunes of the lowly Pirates and rushed Friend to the majors. Rickey watched Friend excel in a spring training game and became wildly enthusiastic about his potential.

"You've got everything you need," Rickey said, "fastball, curve, and change (of speed) on both. Boy, you can be great!"

They were nice words to hear from such a famed magnate of the game, but it took a few years before Friend truly harnessed his control and that helped him swap out losing seasons for winning seasons. Friend gradually evolved into the best starter on the team and remained either at the top of, or near the top of, the rotation for years.

A few years later, though, Rickey appeared to give up on Friend. He informed him that he was going backward, not forward, and Rickey put the pitcher on waivers. Fortunately for the Pirates, no team grabbed him.

Nothing felt better to Friend than his being able to make a major contribution to a team on the rise.

"That's when I learned how to pitch," Friend said of 1955. "I sharpened my fast curve, I improved my control and I developed a change-up. I finally had a clear idea of what I was supposed to do on the mound. I guess I had been on a loser so much I had a defeat-ish attitude."

Once Friend settled into that good grove, personnel around the league noticed.

"A complete pitcher," said Dodger catcher Roy Campanella, the three-time NL Most Valuable Player. "Hasn't even reached his peak."

Cincinnati Reds manager Birdie Tebbetts called Friend "the best pitcher in the National League."

It was a long time coming and took a lot of work, but by the mid-1950s Friend had arrived and concurrently the Pirates' roster was not so thin anymore and they began working their way up in the standings.

"I wouldn't trade Friend for any pitcher in this league," said then-Pittsburgh manager Bobby Bragan in 1957.

During that season Friend took a perfect game into the eighth inning against the Dodgers, but then allowed a single to Junior Gilliam and a home run to Duke Snider and was down a run so quickly it had his head spinning.

"It wasn't until I reached the bench that the shock struck me," Friend said. "That's when I felt as though I just stepped on a booby trap. Perfect game? I'd just lost an imperfect one, 2 to 1."

Despite that special 22-14 season of 1958, though, Friend still had his ups and downs, sandwiching losing seasons around being the league-leader in victories.

Both the Pirates as a group, with the addition of such players as Bill Mazeroski, Dick Groat, Roberto Clemente, and others, and Friend as an individual, kept growing and meshing.

"Then the club made the move into first place and it was all different," Friend said. "I began to figure it out."

Being part of the World Series winners in 1960 was special for every Pirate, but Friend played five more years in Pittsburgh. In Friend's mind he wasn't getting older, he was still getting better. He won 17 games in 1963 with a 2.34 earned run average.

"I'm a better pitcher now than I was four or five years ago," Friend said. "Sure, I don't have the raw stuff I had then, but I don't make the silly mistakes I did then."

Friend completed his career with a 197-230 record, paying the price for those early years in particular, but with a very respectable 3.58 ERA.

Later in life he became an insurance executive, served in public office as Allegheny County controller., and was active in Republican Party politics, all in the Pittsburgh area.

24
RIP SEWELL

Except for a 0-0 rookie appearance with the Detroit Tigers Truett Banks Sewell of Decatur, Alabama and Vanderbilt University played his entire Major League career for the Pirates in the 1930s and 1940s.

Sewell pitched for 13 years and was a three-time All-Star, with his best years coming after a hunting accident limited his throwing and forced a motion adjustment. He invented a blooper pitch unlike anything anyone had seen, though it was surprisingly effective. The "eephus pitch" bizarrely was thrown on a high lob curve that could reach 25 feet in the air, and with its spin left batters confused.

The 6-foot-1, 180-pound righty compiled a record of 143-97 with a 3.48 earned run average.

Sewell, cousin of big leaguers Joe and Luke Sewell, was 25 when he had that sip of coffee with the Tigers, was mired in the minors after that, and was 31 years old in 1938 when the Pirates signed him and used him in 17 games. Sewell was all of 0-1 that year. He had suffered through serious hardships to make it that far, overcoming a childhood speech impediment and the death of his first wife in childbirth.

In 1939, Sewell emerged from the Pittsburgh bullpen and recorded a 10-9 mark, the beginning of a strong stretch for him that propelled his Major League career into his forties. In one game Sewell shut out the New York Giants and also hit a home run.

Sewell was a college student in need of money when he departed the Vanderbilt campus in Nashville, Tennessee for pro ball.

"There was a Depression," Sewell said. "I saw 35 guys with diplomas who couldn't find jobs. That and the $400 a month offer from the (Nashville) Vols, made up my mind."

If people think the knuckleball is an odd pitch, it doesn't even rate within the same area code for weirdness as the eephus pitch. Instead of being thrown straight to home plate, Sewell threw it in an arcing loop. Just like the knuckler, though, it came in to the batter slowly and seemed to be easy to hit. Only it wasn't.

Joe Falls, the veteran Detroit sportswriter for The Sporting News, likened Sewell's tosses to the type more commonly seen in a slow-pitch softball game. Once Sewell discovered he was on to something he got some (presumably stifled) laughs out of watching enemy hitters flail away and create breezes with their swings.

"They'd hit it about as high as the ceiling in this room," Sewell said years into his retirement. "I remember once we were playing the Boston Braves. Eddie Miller, their shortstop, used to go crazy when I'd give him the old eephus. He'd stand there and scream, 'I'm going to get you! I'm going to knock your head off!' Poor Eddie. This one day he couldn't take it any more and he reached out and caught the ball as it came over the plate. He threw it up in the air and hit it with his bat. He lined it right back at me and I caught it up here, in front of my face."

Sewell had only middling success in the bigs until he went to the eephus pitch. He was looking for a new weapon and began goofing around with it in the bullpen. He got to teasing teammates with it in batting practice and none of them got good wood on the ball, either. It was a sign. Al Lopez, the Hall of Famer, was his catcher, and urged Sewell to give it a try in a real game. He first used it in an exhibition. After the game sportswriters demanded to know what was up with the new pitch and what did he call it. Well, Sewell hadn't come up with any kind of pet name.

"I don't have a name for it," Sewell said. "I just throw it."

The answer to the question came from an unlikely source. Outfielder

Maurice Van Robays, a teammate, spontaneously made history. Van Robays said, "It ain't nothin', and that's what this pitch is—nothin'." And Van Robays didn't even have to face the pitch.

Things changed for Sewell. In 1940 he went 16-5 with a 2.80 earned run average. In 1942 he finished 17-15. In 1943 he had his best year, going 21-9. The wins and his 25 complete games led the National League. In 1944 Sewell won 21 games again. He was an All-Star in '43, '44 and 1946. In 1948 Sewell had the NL's best winning percentage at .813 with his 13-3 record. Sewell retired the next year at 42, but was 6-1 even at the end.

One of the most notable incidents involving the eephus pitch occurred in the 1946 All-Star game. Red Sox slugger Ted Williams, a student of hitting, played in the other league and had not faced the pitch. He asked Sewell to throw it if the occasion arose. It did and Williams smashed the ball for a three-run homer to win the game. Sewell described Williams' hit as a "Sunday Super Dooper Blooper."

"Williams laughed all of the way around the bases and I laughed with him," Sewell said. "The fans ate it up."

Although his record shows that Sewell did surrender home runs, even in his best years, it is commonly said that the Williams blast was the only homer anyone ever slugged off of Sewell's eephus pitch. Even rarer than the knuckler, despite Sewell being a willing teacher, he had no followers.

"I tried to teach it to about 50 big-league pitchers, but they just couldn't get the hang of it," he said.

Later in life Sewell, who was afflicted with diabetes, had his legs amputated and used a wheelchair or a cane with artificial limbs to get around, though he didn't let his condition sidetrack his golf game. When the news spread of his affliction Sewell received 200 pieces of supportive mail, including a note from President Richard Nixon. Sewell was 82 when he died in 1989.

"*It wasn't funny when it happened. I run back, back and I don't see ball. Then my head…oh, how it hurt.*"

– Manny Sanguillen

25
MANNY SANGUILLEN

An accidental baseball player virtually drafted into the sport when the native of Panama was attending a Bible school and his team needed a fill-in Manny Sanguillen became a star catcher for the Pirates.

Born in Colon, Panama in 1944, Sanguillen first played baseball in 1964, but by 1967 he made his first appearance in the majors. All but one year of Sanguillen's 13-year Major League career was spent with Pittsburgh and today Sanguillen remains a popular figure at PNC Park where he runs a barbeque stand. Fans can purchase a meal from Sanguillen and also get a free autograph as a side dish.

Sanguillen was a four-time .300 hitter for the Pirates and a three-time National League All-Star. He broke in with the club in 1967 and batted .271 as a rookie.

Notorious for his uncanny ability to hit pitches thrown out of the strike zone, Sanguillen was not a power hitter, but he had seasons for the Pirates when he batted .325, .319, and .328. He was a superb defensive catcher with a strong throwing arm and was a key player when the Pirates fielded some top-notch teams in the early 1970s. Sanguillen was a member of the 1971 World Series champions and was also part of the 1979 championship group.

The son of an electrician, Sanguillen was attending the Pan American Mission school when he took up baseball and learned how to catch. One might say he had a serious learning curve. The first time he attempted to grab a foul pop-up the ball hit him on the head.

"I can laugh about it now," Sanguillen said years later. "It wasn't funny when it happened. I run back, back and I don't see ball. Then my head…oh, how it hurt."

So did the boos that followed, but he worked hard to improve. He made such an impression one of his teacher's made contact on his behalf with Pittsburgh's Latin American scout Howie Haak. Haak saw Sanguillen's potential and signed him.

Sanguillen posted a .296 lifetime average, unusually high for typically overworked catchers. Not only was he quick to protect the plate on defense he was also a pretty fast runner for a catcher. As evidence of the 6-foot, 193-pound Sanguillen's foot speed, manager Danny Murtaugh often batted him second in the lineup. That is very much a rarity for a catcher. In school Sanguillen ran the 100-yard dash for the track team.

Unlike the more typical slower-running catcher, Sanguillen helped the Pirates by being able to routinely score from second base on singles. When someone—the Giants' Ken Henderson--actually nailed him on a throw to the plate from right field, Sanguillen was stunned.

"Never happen before," Sanguillen said in his Spanish-accented English. "Never. Never. First time in my life I was ever thrown out at home. This guy, I guess, he play in. When I look, he was close to second base. I know I'm fast."

Possessing a distinctive catching style, Sanguillen was easy to recognize behind the plate. He kept his right knee on the ground and his left leg stuck out at an angle.

When he first joined the Pirates' organization Sanguillen's English was limited. But the often chatty, open Sanguillen made himself into a talker in a second language. In Batavia, in New York, on his first minor-league team, Sanguillen went to the same restaurant every day and ordered steak every time because that was all he knew how to obtain. Gradually, his vocabulary expanded.

"I buy one dictionary," Sanguillen said.

He used it, too, but also swung a bat that spoke in a universal language. Sanguillen had the knack for hitting the ball into gaps in the defense and teammate Jerry Mays said, "He finds the holes."

Sanguillen became well-regarded as a handler of pitchers with the Pirates, but his early minor-league sessions on the mound with pitchers in difficulty couldn't have helped the throwers too much. Each time he went out to visit a pitcher he said, "Come on baby, throw hard." That may have been the best advice, but it was Sanguillen's only advice. "Those were the only words I knew," he said.

That first season in the majors was only a partial one for Sanguillen—30 games—and he returned to the minors in 1968. But the next season he was back to stay and batted .303. He started the year on such a tear that a couple of weeks into the 1969 campaign Sanguillen was batting .533. He also toted one of the biggest chunks of lumber to the plate since the 1930s when he wielded a 40-ounce bat.

Sanguillen seemed to be a naturally friendly man who laughed often and greeted strangers with a smile. However, he did have some personal challenges. Sanguillen, who is black, married a white woman, and there was some strain between the sides of the family. Sanguillen was also more religious than his wife, and that bothered him.

"My wife has become a serious Christian," Sanguillen said later in his career. "I used to pray for her."

Sanguillen said he had a temper when he was younger, but learned patience and became "a new man" a few years into his Major League career through religion.

Probably Sanguillen's best all-around season was 1971. He hit seven home runs, drove in a career high 81 runs, and batted .319. That year he was voted the best catcher in the National League, an achievement for all of the other years around that Hall of Famer Johnny Bench of Cincinnati captured that rating.

Unlike many more discerning hitters Sanguillen never accumulated many walks. He often swung at outside pitches or low pitches. Haak, the scout that signed him suggested early in Sanguillen's minor-league apprenticeship that he be more aggressive on hurlers' first offerings. That created a monster.

"Now I swing at almost everything," Sanguillen said a few years later. "I think I get a lot of base hits on bad pitches."

That became one of his trademarks.

26
BABE ADAMS

His real name was Charles Adams, but the pitcher who won 194 career games was called Babe. When Babe Ruth pretty much took over the nickname in the 1920s Adams was referred to as "the original Babe."

Born in 1882 in Tipton, Indiana, Adams went to high school in Missouri. He was a right-handed thrower who stood 5-foot-11 and weighed 185 pounds and his reputation was for being stingy in issuing bases on balls.

Adams broke into the majors with the St. Louis Cardinals in 1906 and took one loss. The rest of his career, through 1926, he served the Pirates. Adams twice reached at least 20 victories and had three other seasons of 18, 17, and 17 wins. His lifetime earned run average was a sterling 2.76. His 194 triumphs are the second most in team history.

Ranked high on the Pirates all-time top-10 lists among pitchers, Adams threw 2,991 innings and walked just 430 batters. In 1920, when Adams was 38, he pitched 263 innings and permitted just 18 walks. Now that's control. Overall, Adams allowed 1.38 walks per nine-inning game. He once pitched all 21 innings of a game against Rube Marquard without allowing a walk—yet he lost 3-1. It was also possible that the extraordinary effort caused an injury because Adams' arm was out of sorts for a long while afterwards.

From an early age growing up on a farm Adams worked on his control. He threw rocks at rabbits and he threw baseballs through knotholes in barn walls. Adams was born left-handed, but a childhood accident nearly cut off the little finger on that hand and he switched his throwing to his right hand.

"I was always proud of my ability to get the ball over the plate," Adams said. He cited that 1920 season as perhaps his greatest achievement in accuracy.

Although Adams certainly faced the greatest National League hitters of his time, he did not seem to be particularly impressed by any of them.

"They all look alike to me," he said of opposing batters.

Adams notched a career high in victories in 1914 when he finished 22-12. In 1913 he was 21-10. His most notable accomplishment was winning three games in the 1909 World Series for the Pirates. In accordance with his general philosophy Adams was hardly awed by Ty Cobb when he met the Tigers in that Series.

"The papers were full of stories about Cobb this and Cobb that," Adams said. "All this did was make me try harder. Cobb got only one hit off me and that was in the first game."

Adams' three Series wins were all complete-game efforts and he allowed just five runs in the contests. He also appeared briefly in the Series for the Pirates again in 1925 shortly before he retired.

The story line of the '09 Series was supposed to be star Ty Cobb against Pittsburgh star Honus Wagner, but Adams became the star. The small Missouri town of Mount Moriah, a farm community of perhaps 150 people, always remembered Adams and his exploits and much later named a highway after him as well as building a monument to him.

Adams was the first rookie to win three games in a single Series and his performance so excited Pittsburgh residents that when he won the deciding game the fans poured into the streets of the city and some even carried pictures of Adams that they thrust into the air.

It was a surprise—even to Adams—that he started Game 1 of the Series. The scheduled hurler was Howie Camnitz, but he was laid low by an infection.

As game time approached, with roughly 90 minutes to first pitch, Adams was shooting the breeze with teammates in a relaxed fashion since he didn't expect to get in the game. Manager Fred Clarke approached.

"Clarke was standing there and he threw me the ball," Adams said. Clarke said, "You're it." Adams believed Clarke was joking and had to be told a second time. Adams gave up six hits in a 4-1 game for the win.

One notable thing about Adams' Series success: it was technically his rookie year because he pitched so little in the preceding seasons. He was 12-3 in 1909.

Adams' heyday was during a time period when spring training really put the emphasis on training and whipping the men into shape for the long season. The Pirates held their camp in Hot Springs, Arkansas and did take advantage of the natural springs.

"We would take hot baths in the morning and in the afternoon we would hike about eight miles over those Ozark hills and trot a lot of the way," Adams said. "That put us in shape."

Adams had a 30-win season in the minors, which led him to St. Louis. But that was a mere flirtation with that club not investing any time developing his talent. It was one game and out and a sale to Louisville. The Pirates were the ones with the smarts to hang onto Adams. Adams picked up his nickname of Babe while playing in Denver. Supposedly a woman seeking an autograph told him he had a round face like a baby's. Others suggest that women who took a fancy to his good looks shouted to Adams while he was on the mound, saying, "Oh, you babe!"

After he retired from the Pirates Adams played some more baseball in the minors, and then returned to the home area of Missouri and did some farming. But he then turned to journalism and wrote sports stories. Even as he aged Adams procured assignments as a war correspondent during World War II and the Korean War.

Except for occasional flings for local town teams that invited him out to play once in a while Adams stayed away from live action on the diamond. He spent his free time having a beer with the guys, smoking cigars and sometimes talking baseball. Adams died at 86 in 1968.

> ***The hell with winning a game. I didn't get a hit and that's what counts with me.***
>
> – Kiki Cuyler

27
KIKI CUYLER

Probably more closely identified with the Chicago Cubs, Hazen "Kiki" Cuyler began burnishing his Hall of Fame resume with the Pirates. Cuyler made his first big-league appearance in 1921, but one game was all he got that year. Same in 1922. In 1923 Cuyler made it into 11 contests. But then came four straight first-rate seasons for the Pirates.

Once Cuyler got his seasoning out of the way he became virtually an overnight star. Once the Pirates threw him into the lineup more or less full-time, they received the reward. Cuyler batted .354 with 85 runs batted in, 94 runs scored and 32 stolen bases.

The 5-foot-10, 180-pound outfielder was from Harrisville, Michigan and the more he played the better he got. Cuyler made his home folks proud and in later years they put up a sign reading, "Home of Hazen (Kiki) Cuyler." Cuyler carved out a 17-year career, all in the National League and his .321 lifetime batting average was good enough to get him elected to the Hall of Fame.

Cuyler's nickname of Kiki also dated to his boyhood. People started calling him "Cuy" for short and then repeating it quickly. Cuy, Cuy became Kiki.

In 1925, when the Pirates won the World Series over the Washington Senators, Cuyler had the best season of his lengthy career. He batted .357 with a .423 on-base percentage. It was quite the chore for pitchers to get Cuyler out. He slugged 18 home runs, gathered 220 hits, and drove in 102 runs, while leading the National League with 26 triples and runs scored with 144. It was the kind of statistical line that would make other players drool with envy.

Very early on Cuyler also established a reputation as a fine fielder and one with a cannon arm who was not to be dared running the bases. While Cuyler did not duplicate his across-the-board numbers, in 1926 he did record starry figures. He batted .321 with 92 runs batted in and again led the NL with 113 runs.

In general, Cuyler was known as a friendly player who drank milk shakes, not alcohol, didn't smoke, and was married and didn't keep late hours touring night clubs. Some opponents thought he was such a nice guy that he may have been short on killer instinct, something that prevented him from being a super great.

Although the tale did not emerge for many years, there was one story about Cuyler that cut across the grain of these goody-goody anecdotes. The Pirates won the National League pennant again in 1927 and earned another trip to the World Series, this time to meet the New York Yankees.

After his three phenomenal seasons Cuyler hit .309 in 1927, but only appeared in 85 games. This was not due to a major injury. And when it came to the World Series Cuyler did not play at all. More than a quarter of a century later Hall of Famer Paul Waner told a somewhat fantastical story.

Cuyler was in a slump and Pirates manager Donie Bush wanted to move him around a little in the batting order. Cuyler was superstitious about where he batted and objected. Cuyler played one game in his new spot in the order and went oh-for-five, although the team won. Manager Bush went to console Cuyler—this according to Waner—and said, "Tough luck, Kiki. But don't worry about going hitless. We won our 11th straight and you'll start finding some holes in that outfield."

Having just emerged from the shower Cuyler was drying his body in front of his locker and allegedly said, "The hell with winning a game. I didn't get a hit and that's what counts with me."

That was Waner's account of the exchange. Bush was slow to boil, but then erupted and said to Cuyler, "You have played your last game on this club as long as I am manager."

Cuyler did not play for the rest of the regular season, nor play in the Series. The next year he was a Chicago Cub, where he distinguished himself with a terrific career.

Waner told this story in 1954, four years after Cuyler passed away. Bush lived until 1972, but never gave a reason why Cuyler was benched. At the time he took considerable heat from fans who considered it strange the manager had a .300 hitter sitting on the bench. Some contemporary discussion attributed Cuyler's stint on the bench to a nagging leg injury.

Then it was said that Cuyler got on Bush's bad side because he refused to slide.

"During that season Bush seemed to dislike me for no reason in the world," Cuyler said. "He ordered me to bat second instead of third in the lineup. I said to Bush, 'You're the manager and I'll hit anyplace you say, but I'm not adapted to second place. I am a free swinger and take a long cut at the ball, and therefore miss a lot of swings. Neither can I place a hit as a man in that position should be able to do.' Well, that didn't do any good. Bush told me to bat second just the same."

Cuyler described the tipping point as a play when he went into second base standing up because he thought it would disrupt a throw, but the ball was dropped and he would have been safe if he slid. So he was fined $50 by Bush and benched.

Clearly, there was a problem between Cuyler and Bush whatever form it took and it resulted in a star and future Hall of Famer being exiled to Chicago. Cuyler had suspicions that owner Barney Dreyfuss was behind the difficulties and claimed that he never knew exactly what transpired to fall out of favor and end his tenure in Pittsburgh.

Cuyler was only 50 when he died after a heart attack followed problems with blood clots. Cuyler was chosen for the Hall of Fame 18 years after his death by the Veterans Committee.

> ***I will always remember that I am made of the same stuff as the worst sinner and without God's help I would be worse than he.***
>
> – Vernon Law

28
VERNON LAW

A career Pittsburgh Pirate, right-handed pitcher Vernon Law turned in his finest season on the mound during a season when his team needed him the most and he was amply rewarded for it. In 1960, when the Pirates captured the National League pennant and won the World Series Law was a 20-game winner and was honored with the Cy Young Award.

Born in Meridian, Idaho, Law was 20 when he broke in with the Pirates in 1950. He won seven games as a rookie and he remained with Pittsburgh until 1967. A 6-foot-2, 195-pound hurler, Law compiled a lifetime record of 162-147. His son Vance also played in the majors.

Many teams were after Law in 1948 when he graduated from high school, but some of the scouts were looked at askance for their comparatively uncouth behavior in a religious household—cigar smoking. The Pirates did their homework, sending representatives to talk to Law's parents carrying roses and chocolates and since one of the team's part owners was Bing Crosby, it didn't hurt at all that the crooner phoned in while attempts to woo the pitcher were underway. Crosby even owned a ranch that was not far from the Laws' home.

Law discovered years later that the Pirates out-smarted the competition by having one of their guys pass out the offensive cigars to the competitors. Crosby told Law that himself.

Equipped with an excellent fastball and a solid curve, Law had to establish his control before growing into a more successful Major League pitcher

Law, who finished 18-9 in 1959, was the man of the hour in baseball in 1960 with his 20-9 mark. Law, an elder in the Mormon Church, was always conscious of setting a good example for youngsters who could be influenced by a man in uniform. He did not smoke or drink or swear, though he was as competitive as any other athlete. He also did not believe in professional athletes offering testimonials to tobacco or alcohol products.

"I'm no prude," Law said, "but I just feel an athlete whom the youngsters admired so much should not endorse those products. If they want to smoke and drink, that's all right, but I don't see what good they can accomplish with the kids when they publicize it. Oh, I've puffed on a cigarette and taken a sip of beer, but I didn't like either. Most every kid has tried it once."

Law much preferred having kids emulate his pitching motion and success. He joined the Pirates when they fielded some of the worst teams in club history, but also grew along with the team as the franchise improved year by year in the 1950s.

In 1957 Law finished 10-8. In 1958 he went 14-12. In 1959 he ended up 18-9 and then had the 20-win campaign in '60.

"Just a combination of circumstances kept me from winning two more last season," Law said in 1960. "I made three starts in early May, pitched seven innings twice and nine innings in the other game, yet didn't get a decision."

Law got his 20 that next season—plus the honor of being the ace of a staff that was good enough to win it all in a dramatic Series triumph. All of his good fortune seemed to evaporate the next summer with injury that culminated in a 3-4 record. Law battled to the end of the 1961 season with an injured ankle, but favoring it threw off his motion and he tore shoulder muscles. It was a big comedown. There is nothing worse than a sore arm for a pitcher and there is nothing better than recovering from a sore arm to pitch well again.

"I never realized how much good health means to a person," Law said. "A person with sound health is a very wealthy person. This I found to be true from experience."

It took until 1965 for Law, competing against the odds, to post another top record of 17-9. When Law made that health-related comment it had been five years since his arm was sound. At one point during his tribulations, in 1963, Law announced his retirement. It seemed as if Law was finished. He was 4-5 in a truncated season. But he kept fighting and he was better the next year, winning 12 games. From nowhere to somewhere.

"I didn't know whether the arm would come around or not a year ago," he said in spring training of 1965. "That was the main reason I didn't bring my family with me. If the arm kicked up again I was going back home and would retire."

Law knew it was time to either put up or give up and fortunately for him his arm was at last rejuvenated. It was not easy to get well, but Law's comeback culminated with that fine 17-9 season.

"I never saw a fellow suffer as much as he did when he was trying to pitch his way back," said Pirates trainer Danny Whelan, who worked long hours with Law. "He endured every kind of pain, yet never once complained."

Even at the worst of times during his career Law felt he was a lucky guy because he was a baseball player and that precluded his right to complain.

"I will always remember that I am made of the same stuff as the worst sinner and without God's help I would be worse than he," Law said. "I often bow my head when I'm pitching or even sitting on the bench and say a silent prayer."

Almost impossibly after so many years of problems, Law recorded a 2.15 earned run average in 1965. He won the National League Comeback Player of the Year Award. In 1966 he went 12-8. But when Law finished 2-6 in 1967 he knew it was time to retire. He stayed out of a Pirates uniform for about 10 minutes, soon after his last season being announced as the new pitching coach for 1968.

> “*He was so good at ‘laying down’ the ball that he had a trick of his own whereby he would flip the bat, grab the meat end of the club in his hands and bunt the ball perfectly with the handle of the bat.*
>
> – Ed O’Neill, Courier Post 1971”

29
JAKE BECKLEY

The 5-foot-11, 200-pound first baseman known as "Eagle Eye" was a top player for the Pittsburgh Alleghenys/Pirates starting in 1888 and Jacob Peter Beckley was one of the franchise's first tough competitors of major achievement. Jake Beckley was chosen for the Hall of Fame decades later.

One of Beckley's peculiar habits was the way he shouted "Chickazoola!" to upset opposition pitchers. He had a loud voice and it carried when he yelled out that distracting word. He was a daring player of considerable skill who made sure he had fun playing. Beckley sported a very thick, black mustache.

Beckley was born in 1867 in Hannibal, Missouri and that's where he began playing baseball as a semi-pro star. He threw left and batted left and in his rookie year in Pittsburgh as a 20-year-old Beckley batted .343.

During a 20-year career as Beckley batted .308 he switched teams within the National League a few times, but got off to his strong start with Pittsburgh and spent until 1896 with the team. He batted .300 or higher, 13 times, and developed that trait right away with the Alleghenys/Pirates.

After the flashy high average recorded during his first season in the majors, Beckley followed up with averages such as .301, .324, .303, .345, and .328 in Pittsburgh. However, the .324 average was recorded playing with the Pittsburgh Burghers in the Players League.

Pitchers of his era found it very difficult to strike out Beckley. He might bat about 600 times in a season and strike out perhaps 25 times. No question Beckley earned his moniker "Eagle Eye" for his discerning swing choices at the plate. In 1894 Beckley made 621 plate appearances and struck out 16 times, a truly remarkable performance.

In 1890, Beckley led the NL in triples with 22. Beckley did not often lead the league in any major batting category, but he posted terrific numbers in various statistical categories besides average. In 1892 Beckley stole 30 bases, his career high. Five times with the Pirates Beckley scored more than 100 runs, ranging from 102 to 123. Four times with Pittsburgh Beckley topped 100 RBIs in a season, ranging from 106 to 122.

Beckley was an offensive force for Pittsburgh in many ways. He was versatile and a run producer during the deadball era when home runs were a rarity. The most four-baggers he hit in a season with Pittsburgh was 10.

Beckley was moved to the New York Giants in 1896 during the season, and also played for the Cincinnati Reds and St. Louis Cardinals, which was pretty much a homecoming for the Missouri boy. Beckley was traded to the Giants for Harry Davis, a solid player, but not one in his class, and $1,000. Pittsburgh did not get much value out of Davis.

Another one of Beckley's quirks was his manner of bunting. While he was regarded as one of the best bunters of all time, Beckley culminated those little taps by hitting the ball with a strange approach. When he knew he was going to bunt, he swiftly turned his bat around and hit the ball with the handle. Beckley's theory was that if he used the thin handle the ball definitely wouldn't travel very far, consistent with his intent.

Many years later Brooklyn Dodgers coach John Corriden shrugged when someone reacted with astonishment that Beckley could perform such a feat.

"In our day everybody could bunt perfectly," Corriden said. "Bunting was like breathing. It didn't have to be taught, and never was forgotten."

Beckley was more or less a contemporary of the celebrated writer Mark Twain, and during his years in the majors, Beckley, who continued to make his home in Hannibal, was often called the second most famous person from the town.

Once, as a way of bringing attention to Hannibal, Beckley persuaded Pittsburgh to play an exhibition game there. Beckley was a little bit of a goofball wherever he played, not just in Pittsburgh. When he was with Cincinnati Beckley and his teammates were riding along the street in a carriage and attempted to lord it over the populace after winning a game. Fans on the street did not respond well. They began pelting the players with fruit and vegetables. Beckley caught a tomato in the mouth and a rotten egg splattered against his uniform.

To some degree Beckley's fielding prowess was overshadowed by his hitting and base running, but he was an agile defender of first base. While not a good thrower with a fairly weak arm, Beckley was an impressive glove man. He led the National League first basemen in fielding percentage more than once and six times led the league in putouts. He set records for the most putouts (23,709) at first and most chances (25,505) at first. In a September, 1898 game Beckley set a record of 21 putouts.

Anyone who has been around baseball knows that the hidden ball trick, when the fielder conceals the ball and fools the runner into stepping off the bag only to be tagged, is one of the most embarrassing moments that can befall a player. Beckley was an early practitioner, though with a twist. He hid the ball under one corner of the bag and behaved innocently enough long enough to trick runners into stepping out of their safe zone.

Beckley stayed in the majors until he was 39 in 1907. But Beckley did not leave baseball after he left the majors. He continued to play in the minors for a while and acted as player-manager in such towns as Kansas City, Bartlesville, Oklahoma, Topeka, Kansas and finally, Hannibal. He even did a little bit of umpiring.

The player always had a soft spot for Hannibal and the town

remembered him. It helped that he finished his big-league career in St. Louis. In 1971, when Beckley was inducted into the Hall of Fame, the Hannibal Chamber of Commerce conducted a special ceremony and unveiled a memorial honor to the baseball

> ***They didn't offer me any money, so I went to college.***
>
> – Bill Madlock

30
BILL MADLOCK

Out of his 15 seasons spent in the majors Bill Madlock spent six in Pittsburgh. He made good use of them, winning two batting titles while representing the Pirates and twice being chosen for the National League All-Star team.

A lifetime .305 hitter, Madlock was a 5-foot-11, 180-pound third baseman who was born in 1951 in Memphis, Tennessee and broke into the big leagues in 1973 with the Texas Rangers before reaching stardom with the Chicago Cubs.

Madlock topped .300 in 10 full or partial seasons. He totaled 163 homers in his career, and while he never drove in 100 runs in a season he still knocked home 80 or 90-plus three times. Madlock was also usually good for 15 stolen bases a year.

The savvy-hitting infielder played in 1,806 games and collected 2,008 hits. Most baseball people probably thought of Madlock as a guy who could hit any time, any place. Only Madlock knew how tough it was for him to become a top-notch hitter.

After he had become an accomplished big-league hitter Madlock told people that when he played Little League he couldn't hit and when he played high school baseball he wasn't much of a hitter either. He made a fairly good impression on scouts, anyway, since the St. Louis Cardinals drafted him.

At that point Madlock learned the difference between being drafted and being wanted.

"They didn't offer me any money, so I went to college," Madlock said.

He enrolled at Southeastern Illinois College, but in 1970 was drafted again, this time by the Washington Senators. By then, however, Madlock was married with a child and the $5,000 offered looked like a difference maker in daily life. And Madlock still didn't hit that well.

The same problem plagued him in the low minors, but when his failure to hit for a decent average cost him a position on a higher level team he got angry and buckled down. That was in 1972 after a demotion from AAA to AA. Bingo, the magic arrived in Madlock's bat and he hit .328, earned a ride back to AAA in Spokane and batted .338.

The last stop up the ladder was heading to the majors—the Senators had become the Rangers by then. Madlock hit .351 in limited play with the Rangers in 1973 and then was traded to the Cubs. The Pirates obtained him in 1979 from the San Francisco Giants in a six-player deal.

It was a timely acquisition. Madlock contributed to the National League pennant winners, hitting .328 in 85 games, and collected a World Series ring.

"It was like a dream come true," Madlock said.

Pittsburgh manager Chuck Tannner said that getting Madlock during the season was a huge positive for the Pirates that year.

"We couldn't have won it without him," Tanner said. "It wasn't just his hitting in the stretch. It was everything. His base running...his fielding."

During this period of Madlock's career there was little continuity—something was always happening to disrupt his rhythm. In 1979 it was the trade. In 1980 he injured his left thumb and had trouble gripping the ball. In 1981 a labor action interrupted the season.

"It will go down to the last few days," Madlock predicted of how the race for the NL batting title would play out. "It always does." Of course, this wasn't an "always" kind of year. The season never resumed, the World Series was lost, and Madlock was crowned batting champion.

His .341 average was worthy, but he played in just 88 games.

Pittsburgh definitely valued his contributions. Madlock signed a six-year, $5.4 million contract with the Pirates in 1981, an era when decimal points are in different places on salaries compared to the numbers involved in the 2000s. Madlock was 30 at the time and eligible for free agency. The idea of staying in Pittsburgh appealed to Madlock.

"It wasn't that way with other clubs," Madlock said of the closeness on the Pirates. "If a guy was traded away I didn't feel any personal loss. But with the Pirates it's been different. There's a closeness here and when a teammate is traded, it's like a personal loss."

After Willie Stargell, the Hall of Fame player and leader retired, Madlock was anointed team captain of the Pirates in 1982.

"Nobody will ever replace Pops," Madlock said, using Stargell's nickname. "But I'll try to lead the way he did, by example. I won't be a clown in the club house next year, but we'll stay loose. Nobody will ever replace Pops, but I'll do my best to be a leader."

Madlock batted .319 during that 1982 season and won his fourth batting title in 1983. As he became more comfortable in Pittsburgh and with his growing success buttressing his resume there seemed to be more interest in looking at Madlock as the whole man. "Grit," self-described as "America's Family Newspaper," wrote a feature about Madlock emphasizing his fascination with antiques. And we're not talking about baseball memorabilia here.

As a player, Madlock was nicknamed "Mad Dog" because he played hard and was competitive. Off the field he seemed like a different person altogether, almost as if he possessed a secret identity. Madlock's hobby was collecting antiques such as furniture, clocks, sculpture, art, and statues. In fact, he owned several Picasso art prints.

The origin of Madlock's antiques interest stemmed from missing out on an All-Star game. He used the break to visit Las Vegas and found an antique clock. Once started Madlock began turning up at flea markets and auctions for stuff the way some baseball fans attend collector's shows.

"I'll drive through small towns to look through the antique shops," he said.

However, after Madlock won his last batting title his hitting mysteriously dropped precipitously. In 1985 he was moved to the Dodgers. Madlock retired from the majors after the 1987 season, but played one season in Japan before going into coaching. He has also been a minor-league manager.

31
BARRY BONILLA

At one point early in Barry Bonilla's career with the Pittsburgh Pirates it seemed possible he would become one of the greatest players in team history. Things didn't turn out that way, but at his best he was very good.

Born in New York, Bonilla was a third baseman (a reluctant one) and outfielder for the Pirates after breaking into the majors with the Chicago White Sox, which no one remembers. He appeared in 75 games for Chicago in 1986.

Bonilla was originally drafted by the Pirates in 1981 when he was 18. In 1985 the White Sox plucked him from Pittsburgh in the Rule 5 draft and after playing half a season for the White Sox he was traded back to Pittsburgh for Jose DeLeon in the midst of the 1986 campaign. That made three times the Pirates chased down Bonilla and obtained his rights.

The 6-foot-3, 230-pound switch-hitter played six years for the Pirates and became a four-time All-Star. He hit .300 or better twice, drove in 100 runs or more three times and twice scored at least 100 runs. He also three times hit at least 24 home runs with a high of 32.

"Some guys are really good at hitting home runs," Bonilla said. "I don't have that. Maybe with time and with consistency I'll get the knack."

Bonilla's first full year in Pittsburgh he batted .300 with 15 home runs and 77 RBIs and the fans who had not been paying attention as Bonilla shuffled in and out of the organization suddenly fell in love with him. He gave a lot of credit to Pittsburgh hitting instructor Milt May for helping him.

Of Puerto Rican heritage, Bonilla grew up in the South Bronx, a short subway ride from Yankee Stadium. The heroes he emulated when he first learned to swing a bat were Tommie Agee and Chris Chambliss. He was primarily a stickball player, but the opportunities he had that approximated baseball were softball and spongeball—hitting a rubber ball.

Neighborhood crime was a major problem, but Bonilla's father, previously an inner city stickball-spongeball star, kept a tight leash and influence on Bonilla.

"My dad (an electrician) taught me there's a lot of worse things I could be doing," Bonilla said.

One of four children, Bonilla's parents divorced when he was eight. The community offered such sights as people being shot and shooting up heroin.

While his family emphasized straight behavior and Bonilla embraced sports, the translation gap between stickball and hardball in the pros was a yawning gap. Bonilla may have been talented, but it took a considerable time for him to adjust to the faster speed of the game in the minors. He had seasons where he batted. 217 and .228 in the Pirates' organization, but that kept him buried in the low minors.

"I was a baby in a lot of things, trying to learn how to cope with not being home," Bonilla said.

Once Bonilla matured and fine-tuned his skills he became one of the top players on the team as the 1980s ended and the 1990s began. Bonilla's 1990 season was a special one. Although his batting average settled at .280 he hit 32 home runs, drove in 120 runs, and scored 112.

Certain players throughout baseball history have been known for playing the game with a smile on their face and it was important to Bonilla that those watching him realized he was one of them and that he reveled in being out on the field.

"I love this game," Bonilla said. "I always have. When it stops being fun, then it's time to do something else. If you're not having fun, it's hard to put up the numbers."

Bonilla was pretty hot stuff in 1991, too. He raised his average to .302. He hit 18 home runs, drove in 100 runs and scored 102. He also led the National League in doubles with 44. The biggest issue for the Pirates was that Bonilla's contract was up and as a free agent coming off four consecutive All-Star selections he was in position to command a huge contract. Pittsburgh team officials did not believe they could compete on the open market for Bonilla's services. As the 1991 season was coming to an end there was considerable speculation about Bonilla's future.

The Pirates put such offers on the table as $13.5 for three years and $16.8 million for four years, but Bonilla had not accepted. Bonilla said he refused to let the impending negotiations distract him.

"No, because I want to have nothing but fond memories of my career," Bonilla said. "You can't let stuff like contract negotiations bother you, because I make a lot of money now. I have no fuss about that. The point is either they want me here or they don't. It's a choice that they have to make. All I can do is be Bobby Bonilla and play the best baseball that I can play as an individual."

Bonilla was playing excellent baseball and so were his teammates. The 1991 Pirates finished 98-64 and won the National League East. Among Bonilla's teammates were Barry Bonds. Pittsburgh was one of the best teams in baseball and seemed likely to remain among them as long as the Pirates retained their top players.

"I think people have enjoyed the way I play and that's what I want them to enjoy," Bonilla said. "I want them to say, 'Bobby Bonilla had a lot of fun playing and that's what we enjoyed watching.'"

That may have been Bonilla's professed attitude, but the Pirates lost the NL Championship Series to the Atlanta Braves four games to three and Bonilla never played another game for Pittsburgh. He left as a free agent to sign with his hometown New York Mets. Bonds left for the San Francisco Giants and that gutted the core of the offense. The Pirates declined and tumbled into a two-decade tailspin because of an inability to compete financially for star players.

32
SMOKY BURGESS

Owning one of the great nicknames in sports history, one which made him sound like a country and western singer, Smoky Burgess didn't really have the build of an athlete. He was somewhat rotund, but he handled a bat with such brilliance that when he wasn't playing regularly Burgess was the best pinch-hitter around.

Born in Corleen, North Carolina in 1927, Forrest Harrill Burgess became a big-league ball player who made his debut in 1949. Burgess played 18 years in the majors, competing for five clubs and compiled a .295 career batting average. Probably his finest years were representing the Pirates.

Burgess did not become a Pirate until 1959 when he was 32. He played five seasons-plus in a Pittsburgh uniform and hit well every year, including 1960 when he was part of the World Series champions.

As a player who stood about 5-foot-8 and weighed 185-plus pounds, Burgess did not have a classic athletic build and he was slow afoot. However, he was a feared hitter and for Pittsburgh he batted .297, .294, .303, .328, and .280. In all, Burgess was a nine-time All-Star. Some years there were two All-Star games and Burgess was chosen for both. That meant Burgess was on an All-Star team as a Pirate all but two of those nine occasions. It may surprise some that he also led National League catchers in fielding percentage three times.

Burgess was a tremendous pinch-hitter who even when he was not in the lineup on a given day might be the player to determine the outcome of a game. Burgess retired with a Major League record 145 pinch hits (broken by Manny Mota). That was the equivalent of a season's worth of hits.

Burgess was a disciple of Ted Williams' theory about the challenges of hitting a baseball during a game when a pitcher was trying to get a hitter out.

"Ted's absolutely right when he says hitting a round ball squarely with a round bat is the most difficult feat in sport," Burgess said. "If you stay within your limits, it can be accomplished."

Burgess was successful often enough as a pinch-hitter that he had supreme confidence whenever a manager called upon him and he went into a game cold. Many players said they couldn't do it, stepping in on short notice in the middle of a game without warm-ups. Not Burgess. Eventually he became so comfortable at the plate and acquired such a good reputation that he felt his mere presence was putting the pressure on the pitcher.

"Most people think the pressure's on the batter when he's up there to pinch-hit," Burgess said. "But my reputation for coming through in the clutch put the pressure on the pitcher."

Burgess did not obtain many bases on balls. The most number of games he ever played in was 123, and so he knew he had to take advantage of every time up at the plate to create some action.

"I always went up there swinging," Burgess said, indicating he was not someone who was going to stand at the plate and just gaze at a pitcher's first offering. "I wasn't looking for any walks. My job was to drive in runs, not to leave it up to the next guy. Rarely did the count get to three-and-two when I was batting. If the pitch was within reach I'd hack away. I'd spend my time on the bench studying the pitcher, watching how he handled teammates of mine whose batting style was similar to the way I batted."

Only twice during his career did Burgess bat more than 400 times in a season. It was almost as if he was a secret weapon called out for specific circumstances, or a fine wine only to be opened for special occasions. There were times Burgess felt he should have been a team's full-time catcher, but was not given a fair shot in his mind or given the job. But he always responded with fine play when invited into the line-up. He brought the same attitude to the plate if he was skipped when All-Star squads were picked and he believed he was deserving.

"I can catch at least 100 games a year and after that I should be good for pinch-hitting until I'm 40," Burgess said.

The burly receiver did have trouble holding down his weight. He was 185 some of the time, 188 part of the time, and as his career went on he gained weight and nearly hit 200. Burgess said he was actually kind of a skinny dude when he was younger before going into the military.

"I gained all my weight while I was in the Army," he said. "I was in charge of the post office and had a good friend who was a mess sergeant. At night we would visit the kitchen and he kept filling me up on everything fattening. I'll bet I gained 30 pounds in the Army and the weight just stayed with me."

In 1967, when Burgess, who also played for the Phillies, was still doing some serious swinging, the Philadelphia Bulletin ran a headline reading "Everyone Loves a (.300-Hitting) Fat Man." The occasion of the story was an honor bestowed upon him by "Fat Fathers Of America." Burgess, who wore a 44 sport coat, was chosen for the award for "contributions toward dignifying the role of the overweight man in contemporary life."

Burgess admitted "I'm heavier than I should be, but I wouldn't say I'm one of these here that's really soft like a lot of people that's really fat. I've always said there's two different types of fat people—ones that will admit it and ones that won't. I'll admit I'm fat."

He also had serious problems with ulcers and played through that issue. The 1967 season was Burgess' last at 40 with the White Sox. Later, Burgess was voted into the Cincinnati Reds Hall of Fame. He was 64 when he passed away in Asheville, North Carolina.

Courtesy of the National Baseball Hall of Fame Library

A three-time Pirate All-Star, **Al Oliver** was a reliable .300 hitter whether he played the outfield or first base.

33
AL OLIVER

A native of Portsmouth, Ohio, Al Oliver was born in 1946 and made his Major League debut with the Pirates in 1968 when he appeared in four games. He spent 10 years with Pittsburgh and while representing the Pirates he was a three-time All-Star and topped .300 four times.

Oliver's real rookie year—when he was runner-up for the rookie of the year honors—was in 1969 when he cracked 17 home runs, drove in 70 runs and batted .285. It was the kickoff to a first-rate career. The first impressive stretch of Oliver's big-league career was in Pittsburgh but he excelled elsewhere, as well.

Over 18 seasons outfielder-first baseman Oliver batted .303, batted at least .300 12 times, was a seven-time All-Star, and won the 1982 National League batting crown for the Montreal Expos.

The 6-foot, 195-pound lefty swinger was a tough out from the time he came up through the Pirates system until his retirement in 1985. He also bashed 219 home runs and drove in 1,326 runs and collected 2,743 hits. Pittsburgh fans probably wish that Oliver spent his entire career in the Steel City. In 1977 Oliver was part of a complicated, four-team, multi-player trade that brought Bert Blyleven and John Milner to Pittsburgh.

"I didn't want to be traded," Oliver said. "I would have loved to have spent 18 years in Pittsburgh. It would have been great."

Oliver's four games in 1968 was just a soak-it-all-in cameo, but it didn't take long in 1969 for Oliver to become a well-respected player. He was not the best fielder in the league. He was not the biggest home-run hitter. What Oliver did for the Pirates was make them a better team when he took his position. Very early in his career, minor league manager Johnny Pesky, the former Major League shortstop, gleaned that insight watching Oliver play every day.

"Oliver is the kind of ball player who grows on you," said Pesky, who managed Oliver in AAA. "Forget his average, forget his ability to play first base so well. You can forget almost everything except that Oliver is the type ball player who helps you win ball games."

That was probably the best description ever made of Oliver's all-around contributions.

Pesky was a good judge of talent. He played with Boston Red Sox Hall of Famers Ted Williams and Bobby Doerr. He watched Oliver's development closely as he climbed through the minor-league levels, and he proved himself an astute judge when analyzing how Oliver would fare.

"Left-handers won't stop the kid," Pesky said. "When he his hitting, he will hit everybody. Once in a while he falls into the over-swinging habit, but it won't last. Know why? Because he is the type who will listen and take instruction."

Oliver earned a full-time job for the Pirates coming out of spring training in 1969, but he did have some early adjustment problems facing big-league hurling every day. As the weather heated up, so did Oliver, and he gained confidence.

"I won't strike out a lot if I play every day," Oliver said. "I generally make contact."

That was not arrogance, but accuracy. Oliver never did strike out a lot during his career. He had several seasons with the Pirates when he came to bat 500 or 600 times and struck out only about 35 times.

Not much happened on the diamond that held Oliver back once he became a starter, but an unexpected allergy attack almost did him in once during that 1969 season. Before the game Oliver ate a few pieces of cake. What he didn't know was that nuts were in the cake--and he had an extreme sensitivity to them from the time he was a youngster.

"When it came to game time I felt OK, but a few minutes after the game started I was out at first base and I was itching and sweating and I felt dizzy," Oliver said.

Oliver played out half the inning, but his condition deteriorated. He was helped into the locker room and given treatment by the Pirates' trainer.

"While I was on the table, I passed out," Oliver said. "My pulse, they tell me, became very weak."

The Pirates hustled a doctor into the clubhouse from the stands to help Oliver and it was a scary moment.

"The few players who saw me lying on the trainer's table thought I was dying," Oliver said. "I guess I was, too. Finally, I was given some kind of a needle to snap me out of it. I didn't know the cake had nuts in it. They must have crushed them up in the flour of the cake."

Oliver had been a first baseman, but eased into the role of center fielder. He never got swept up in the temptation of swinging for the fences—14, 17, 18, 20, those were the types of home-run numbers Oliver put up each year.

"Some fellows get a kick out of hitting home runs," Oliver said. "My big thrill is just hitting the ball on the nose."

Gradually, Oliver evolved from a guy asserting himself in the lineup to an indispensable player who grew into prominence. By 1973 Oliver was saying that he hoped he could help replace Clemente who had died in 1972 in a plane crash.

"Most people feel I can fill that type of role," Oliver said. "All the players respect me. We get along. They know when I say something I mean it. They all know I can play. Like Clemente, I'm not a drinker, not a smoker. I'm dedicated."

In 1974 Oliver won the Roberto Clemente Award for being a player who "most exemplifies the standards of excellence" established by Clemente.

Oliver was a good all-around athlete who considered going pro in basketball instead of baseball, but watching giants Bill Russell and Wilt Chamberlain dominate the NBA gave him pause.

"I said I'd rather take my chances with a Bob Gibson slider or a Tom Seaver fastball," Oliver said.

34
TONY PENA

When Tony Pena was a young player growing up in the Dominican Republic he was an outfielder. He eventually found his calling as a catcher. Much like Manny Sanguillen, another prominent Pirates catcher, Pena did not merely squat behind the plate, but caught the game with one leg extended establishing a different form of balance.

Pena first absorbed the Panamanian's catching approach when he saw him play in winter ball.

Born in 1957, Pena's full name is Antonio Francisco Pena Padilla. It would never have fit into a headline when Pena struck game-winning bashes.

Pittsburgh signed Pena to an amateur free agent contract in 1975 when he was 18. Pena grew up in the Pirates' organization and made his first Major League appearances in 1980. By then Pena was married and the father of a child. Although he played just eight games, Pena gained notice by hitting .429.

It is an understatement to suggest that the Pirates gushed about Pena's potential from the start.

"It's just a matter of time before Pena is recognized as one of the outstanding catchers," manager Chuck Tanner said in 1981.

That year Tanner platooned Pena and Steve Nicosia (after trading Ed Ott). Tanner used his authority to give both players opportunities and told the Pittsburgh sportswriters that he had two first-string catchers. But along the way it became clear that Pena was going to be the Pittsburgh receiver of the future. He also seemed to have a good handle on what he needed to do to earn the first-string job for keeps.

"I will be better next year because of the experience I got this year," Pena said after that '81 campaign. "When the season started I wasn't sure how I was going to be used. I made some mistakes."

One thing that impressed baseball people about Pena's tools was his strong arm. He routinely gunned down runners trying to steal second base. Pena's sound instincts around the plate also earned him kudos from opposing National League managers who saw him play for the first time.

"He looks like an excellent prospect," said Atlanta Braves manager Bobby Cox.

Pena fixed his mistakes pretty quickly. He was a good hitting catcher and an even better fielding catcher. The 6-foot, 175-pound Pena stayed with the Pirates through the 1986 season. During his time with the club he was a four-time All-Star and three-time Gold Glove winner. He batted .300 twice with Pittsburgh.

Pena became admired as a very durable catcher. In the 2000s catchers are babied a little bit more, playing fewer games at the position and often in the American League play as designated hitters on select days, a quasi-rest at the plate. Pena was an Iron Man by comparison. For several years running in the early 1980s Pena caught 138 games, 151 games, 147 games, and 147 games. There really was no need for a back-up catcher that year except maybe helping out in the bullpen.

The prevailing theory now is that a catcher needs more rest. It has also been suggested that few catchers can uphold the dual load of calling a good game and hitting for a good average. Pena personally debunked that opinion with the combination of catching most of the games, but also hitting well. At the same time that Pena was accepting the huge work load in the field he was hitting at a good clip.

While Pena was one of the catchers who could play every day and still hit he did so across the board. In 1982 Pena batted .296 with 11 home runs and 63 runs batted in. In 1983 his totals were 15 homers, 70 RBIs, .301 average. In 1984 Pena's line read 15 home runs, 78 runs batted in with a .286 mark.

In 1985 Pena kept up his usual pace of playing in 147 games, again with 15 homers and 78 runs batted in. However, for the first time Pena saw slippage in his average, falling to an-un-Tony-like .249. It was apparently deemed to be un-Pirate-like, as well. All seemed to be well in 1986 when Pena hit 10 home runs, drove in 52 and bounced back to .288.

But it wasn't. Pena was aging and the Pirates traded him to the St. Louis Cardinals for Mike Dunne, Mike LaValliere, and Andy Van Slyke (who was in his prime and starred for Pittsburgh). Pena played many more years for four more teams.

Pena's son Tony became a big-league pitcher, but Pena said he got some of his talent and advice from his mother more than his father, who did not play baseball.

"She was a real All-Star," Pena said. "She played softball and she pitched and hit better than most of the men."

One of the earlier generation of Dominican players to make a splash in the big leagues, Pena said baseball was always his number one thing.

"I would love this game, even if I wasn't getting paid to play," Pena said.

Pena was paid to play and he was also paid to watch Major League games after he retired at 40 following 18 seasons. In 2002, Pena became the manager of the Kansas City Royals, a job he retained until 2005.

In 2005 Pena was selected to become manager of the Dominican Republic for the World Baseball Classic.

Coaching his home country's squad in such a prestigious event Pena had a deep and skilled pool of players to choose from in making out the roster. Many of the best players in the majors were Dominican natives and would be eligible to play in the tournament if they wanted to do so. It was not a shortage of talent, but a matter of picking the right players and blending them.

"No one will be out when we choose our roster," Pena said. "I prefer a rookie in top condition over an out-of-shape star anytime."

Pena also went on to spend several years as a coach for the New York Yankees.

35
ANDY VAN SLYKE

Before Andy Van Slyke joined the Pirates he played a little bit of everything in the field. But once Van Slyke locked into center field he became a huge presence, winning five Gold Gloves for Pittsburgh and earning three All-Star berths.

Born in 1960 in Utica, New York Van Slyke was first property of the St. Louis Cardinals and he played the first four seasons of his 13-year Major League career for St. Louis starting in 1983. His greatest success, however, came during his eight seasons with the Pirates. The Pirates obtained Van Slyke in the trade that sent catcher Tony Pena to the Cardinals.

On his way to a lifetime batting average of .274, the lefty swinging Van Slyke was a better fielder than hitter, but he did have his batting moments. Van Slyke's finest season with the Pirates was 1992 when he led the National League in hits with 199 and doubles with 45, and batted .324.

That season Van Slyke was a leader of a Pittsburgh team that finished 96-66 and finished first in the NL East. That was the last Pirates playoff team until 2013.

The higher average that year was partially attributable to the urging of Van Slyke's coaches who wanted him to stop trying to pull every pitched ball. The message came from hitting instructor Milt May who said, "There is something out there called left-field. Use it."

By that point in his career Van Slyke had come a long way from a prospect to a maybe to an All-Star. He had also firmly established an identity in the team clubhouse as the guy most likely to horse around, make jokes, and make others laugh.

Once, Van Slyke was asked if he was able to switch places with anyone else in the world for one day whom would he pick. Most people say such things as the president, a famous actor or superstar athlete. Van Slyke said, "My wife. So I could see how wonderful it is to live with me."

It was not always as wonderful to live with Van Slyke, the beginning of his Major League career being one such time period when he exercised a temper a bit too often and when he wasn't yet at the peak of his game. The Cardinals wanted Van Slyke to play third base, which is not something he believed he had in him. He said, "They wanted me to play third base like Brooks (as in Brooks Robinson). So I did play like Brooks—Mel Brooks."

Van Slyke's real breakthrough from an average player to a star can probably be traced to the 1988 season. He led the NL in triples with 15. He hit 25 home runs. He scored 101 runs and knocked in 100 while batting .288. That season he received his first All-Star and Gold Glove recognition.

An insightful man, as well as a humorous one, Van Slyke never seemed overly impressed with himself, nor with the value of a professional baseball player to society. Teachers deserve more praise than he did, he felt.

"What I do, I don't think is extraordinary," Van Slyke said. "It just happens to be what I do well. But what I find extraordinary is being able to keep 15 five-year-olds' attention for a morning and teach them something. I don't deny that I have a gift. It's just that diving after a baseball doesn't seem to be as extraordinary as being good at something like being a teacher. I enjoy being me. I know who I am. I know the imperfections I have. I know what I don't like about myself. I also know I have good qualities. I magnify them and make the other things vanish from my life. I'm not asking to be perfect. I'm asking God's help to be my water purifier."

Overall during his time with the Pirates, Van Slyke had two seasons of scoring at least 100 runs, three of driving in at least 80 runs, and in just one other season he batted .300--310. His defense was always strong.

"Good defensive outfield play is the most underrated thing in all of the sport," Van Slyke said. "The impact of a great defensive play is more devastating to a team than one made by an infielder."

Van Slyke made himself sound like a basketball star seeking a pass for a last-second shot to win the game as he stood around on the outfield grass waiting for a play to unfold.

"The thing is, you got to want the ball at the moment that counts," he said. "When there's a runner in scoring position I'm out there begging for the ball… 'Let him hit me a one- or two-hopper, please.' I live for the moment where I can change the course of a game."

Pirate officials felt that Van Slyke might thrive in Pittsburgh, but when they acquired him in that multi-player trade they really didn't know that he was such a special defensive player. After watching him for a little while, however, they gushed with compliments.

"I think he's the best center fielder in the league," said Pittsburgh manager Jim Leyland.

With the Cardinals Van Slyke was mostly a part-timer, but stepping into the lineup full-time in Pittsburgh gave him a chance to blossom. He patrolled center next to Barry Bonds in left.

"He can play center field with anyone," Bonds said. "Somebody missed something over there (St. Louis)."

It was Van Slyke's respect for Willie Mays' defense that pushed Van Slyke into asking for an autograph when he had never done so around any other Hall of Fame player.

"I never saw him play," Van Slyke said of Mays, "but I heard he was the best."

Van Slyke played with the Pirates in good times, but also in bad. By 1994, they were looking at last, not first, though as usual he was philosophical.

"You can't expect Mr. Ed to keep up with Secretariat," Van Slyke said.

36
JASON KENDALL

Most of the good stuff that happened to Jason Kendall during his 15-year Major League career occurred with the Pittsburgh Pirates, starting with his rookie year in 1996 as a 22-year-old.

Kendall alerted the baseball world to his presence immediately as a rookie. Kendall batted .300 and made the All-Star team his first season, making for a memorable start with the Pirates. During the nine years Kendall spent catching for Pittsburgh the 6-foot, 180-pound receiver was a three-time All-Star.

Most impressively, and somewhat unusually for a catcher, Kendall was a supremely tough out, hitting at least .300 six times. Many of those years his final average was far higher than .300. During his early years with the Pirates Kendall had such terrific hitting years as .327 in 1998, .332 in 1999, .320 in 2000, and .325 in 2003.

"Jason's a good player," said then-manager Jim Leyland. "He's one of those players who doesn't come along very often."

The 1999 achievement was tempered by it being accomplished in a short season. Kendall, then 25, was injured and played in just 78 games. Kendall was doing something a lot of catchers don't even attempt—he lay down a bunt and was trying to beat it out. That's because Kendall was much faster than the average catcher, sometimes hitting leadoff and regularly stealing bases. He had as many as 26 steals in a season.

Kendall's goal was not merely to get a base hit, but to break up a no-hitter. However, Kendall's spikes caught on the side of first base and he broke and dislocated his right ankle, tearing ligaments, too.

Catchers are often dinged up from foul balls, but this was not something that could be shrugged off in order to play again the next day.

"This is the first time that I've been knocked down to stay," Kendall said. "I saw the replays, but I was in the hospital and not feeling real good, so I watched them but I don't think it really hit me. But I know it was very disgusting."

The damage was so extreme that teammates turned their heads away and Kendall was taken directly from the ball park into surgery.

Gene Lamont, by then the Pirates' manager, told Kendall not to watch the replay, but he watched it over and over again on baseball shows, so that he would never make the same mistake again. There was some question about whether Kendall would be the same again. Some thought he might give up stealing bases, but he said that wasn't going to happen.

"I've got a bionic ankle," he said. "I've got a little titanium screw in there. I can probably play golf with my foot."

If such an exhibition took place it was out of the limelight. However, Kendall did steal 15 or more bases in a season with some regularity again.

Kendall became the first Pirates player to hit for the cycle on May 19, 2000 at Three Rivers Stadium against the St. Louis Cardinals.

Kendall grew up in Torrance, California where he had a 43-game high school hitting streak. His father Fred was a 12-year major leaguer between 1969 and 1980, so baseball was definitely in his blood. He was introduced to the game young and it seemed preordained that he would pursue it. He never expected a setback like the gruesome ankle injury, though, not a simple one to bounce back from. Baseball had to be very special to Kendall because by instinct, especially having grown up in Southern California, his first leaning would have been to become a beach boy. Not a member of the Beachboys singing group, but just a guy who hangs out in sand and ocean with his surf board.

"I'd probably spend my whole life on a beach," Kendall said.

Instead he devoted it to batting cages and ball parks. And in case listeners thought Kendall was kidding, his teammate and friend Al Martin chimed in. Apparently Martin knew Kendall very well. "If not for baseball," Martin said, "he'd be a bum."

Kendall was hardly a laissez-faire dude on the diamond. No one would have guessed that his true self was hidden under the armor catcher's wear and that only half of him was a hardcore competitor. Competing in a sport, though, that was the case.

"I want to beat your ass," Kendall said. "I'm going to do anything I can to beat you."

While it was particularly unusual to see a catcher batting leadoff, Kendall said too much was made of it.

"Hey, I'm happy as long as I'm not hitting ninth," he said.

Kendall was too valuable for that.

It seemed possible that Kendal would remain with the Pirates forever, but in 2004 he was traded to the Oakland Athletics for Mark Redman, Arthur Rhodes and money.

> ***Every boy has the desire to play in the major leagues and I got to play in my hometown.***
>
> – Frank Thomas

37
FRANK THOMAS

The power hitter named Frank Thomas is not the one scheduled to be inducted into the Hall of Fame in 2014. But this Frank Thomas did well for himself, too, especially with the Pirates.

Born in Pittsburgh in 1929, this Thomas, not to be confused with the Chicago White Sox's Thomas of more recent vintage, broke into the majors in 1951 with the Pirates. The 6-foot-3, 200-pound Thomas was primarily an outfielder, but wherever the righty swinger played he made his presence known from the batter's box.

When Thomas was growing up there was no high school baseball at his school, so he played softball. He had already committed to the idea of studying to become a priest and he joined a seminary. It was not until he second-guessed himself and decided he was not going to become a priest that he took up baseball. First it was semi-pro and then he played for a group called the "Little Pirates."

Thomas had just 41 games of baseball experience when a Major League scout made a small bonus offer. He referred to that combination of facts as "the big miracle." However, Thomas preferred the Pirates and he offered them a deal.

"So I told the Pirates I'd sign with them if they'd pay off the mortgage on my dad's home," Thomas said. "They did and I've belonged to them ever since."

Thomas belonged to the Pirates between 1951 and 1958 and he was a three-time All-Star. He was also the most reliable power hitter on the team once Ralph Kiner was traded to the Chicago Cubs. After limited play in 1951 and 1952 in 1953 Thomas slugged 30 home runs and drove in 102 runs.

Over the next several seasons, despite playing in extra-large Forbes Field, Thomas smacked 23, 25, 25, and 23 homers and then culminated his production in 1958 with 35 home runs and 109 RBIs. He hit three one day against the Cincinnati Reds in Crosley Field in August of that season.

"Hitting those three in one game at Cincinnati is absolutely the greatest thrill of my career," Thomas said at the time.

The homer trifecta gave Thomas six runs batted in, which was not a career high. In June of the same season against the Giants he drove in seven runs.

While Thomas was the big gun in the Pittsburgh lineup, the Pirates traded him anyway, to Cincinnati, in early 1959. Thomas was missed, but the Pirates got the best of the deal, solidifying their roster for the 1960 title run with the acquisition of catcher Smoky Burgess, pitcher Harvey Haddix, and third baseman Don Hoak.

Thomas was even on the cover of Sports Illustrated during that gem of a 1958 season.

"Every boy has the desire to play in the major leagues," he said, "and I got to play in my hometown."

Many good things happened for Thomas in '58. On his 29th birthday Thomas mashed a grand slam homer against the Giants—that was in the seven-RBI game.

"Best birthday present I ever had," Thomas said.

That was right after the Giants and Dodgers moved West and settled into ball parks that were considerably friendlier to power hitters than Forbes Field.

"I like to hit in this park," Thomas said of San Francisco. "In fact, I like to hit in Los Angeles, too. I think I'd have a chance to break Babe Ruth's home-run record if I played 77 games in Los Angeles."

In all, Thomas played for 16 years in the majors and hit 286 home runs. He had two 100-RBI seasons, though he never hit .300. More than 55 years after Thomas last played for the Pirates, his 163 homers for the club still ranked seventh on the franchise's all-time list.

During his playing days Thomas regularly visited ill children in hospitals. It was known that he enjoyed the music of Bing Crosby, Eddie Fisher and Jo Stafford among others, and that he did not watch much television because he wanted to protect his batting-eye sharpness. Years earlier famed hitter Rogers Hornsby refused to attend movies for the same reason.

In retirement he worked nearly two decades for the ICM School of Business in Pittsburgh and he and his wife volunteered for many years for Meals on Wheels, delivering food to the needy in the Pittsburgh area.

Thomas, unusual among star players, also had an in-depth baseball card collection. And although he initially thought he would become a priest, not a baseball player, Thomas was like other kids in thinking he would enjoy nothing more than pulling on the home colors.

"Baseball has always been in my blood," Thomas said, "and living so close to Forbes Field naturally made me an ardent Pirate rooter. I had always hoped to play at Forbes Field."

> ***He's a younger player and he's been on championship teams, has a great makeup, and plays hard.***
>
> – General Manager Cam Bonifay

38
BRIAN GILES

Drafted by the Cleveland Indians in 1989, Brian Giles made it to the majors with the Tribe in 1995, but really thrived after being traded to the Pirates in 1999. In five seasons with Pittsburgh the left-handed hitting and throwing outfielder never hit lower than .298.

Giles was born in El Cajon, California in 1971 and his swap to Pittsburgh for Ricardo Rincon gave his career new life. Giles became a two-time All-Star for Pittsburgh, starting strongly with a terrific 1999 season when he batted .315 with 39 home runs and 115 runs batted in.

That welcome-to-Pittsburgh season triggered a run of first-class seasons for Giles. In 2000 he hit 35 home runs, drove in 123 runs, and batted .315. In 2001 Giles hit 37 home runs and knocked in 95 runs while batting .309. In 2002 he hit 38 homers and produced 103 RBIs while batting .298.

And then, about two-thirds of the way through the 2003 season Giles was traded to the San Diego Padres, essentially his hometown team. At that point he had 16 homers, 70 RBIs and a .299 average.

Initially, Giles was disappointed to be traded away from Cleveland because that was the only team he ever knew. His wife cried when he was swapped. Giles was renowned for his practical jokes so his first problem was even convincing her that he was telling the truth. He had fabricated similar stories before. This was a guy who jumped out of a birthday cake naked in a clubhouse and another time told everyone he had been bitten by a scorpion. Giles liked seeing people's reactions.

Arrival in Pittsburgh in 1999 opened worlds of opportunity for Giles and he very much liked the reactions he instigated.

"It was great over in Cleveland, but it gets old when it looks like you're going to get the opportunity each year and you keep getting pushed back to the fourth outfielder," he said. "I just haven't had the opportunity to get 600 plate appearances and see what happens. I felt like I was kind of rotting there."

As soon as Giles and the Pirates saw what happened everyone was pretty happy.

"We needed left-handed power and Brian Giles was a perfect fit," said Pittsburgh general manager Cam Bonifay. "He's a younger player and he's been on championship teams, has a great makeup, and plays hard."

Over a three-year span Giles never scored fewer than 109 runs. The 5-foot-11, 195-pound Giles developed some of his running skills on a football field, though he was smaller at the time and realized he was never going to be a big guy in that game that rewards size.

"When the players started being twice as big as me and were running faster than me, I shut that down real quick," Giles said of the end of his football-playing days.

Giles, whose brother Marcus also played in the majors, became a genuine star in Pittsburgh when he became a full-time player. Teammate Jason Kendall enjoyed playing with Giles and waiting to see what he did next on the diamond.

"He's a good one," Kendall said. "He's fun to watch every day. You never know what you're going to get out of him. He could hit a 500-foot home run or line a ball over the shortstop's head."

The difference between Giles as an Indian and Giles as a Pirate was the difference between platooning and having the trust of management to play every day.

"It seemed like every other week there was a trade rumor when I was in Cleveland," Giles said. "I guess eventually it was going to happen.

I just think it takes a little bit to sink in before you believe."

Giles made the players and fans believe in him pretty quickly.

"He's a Pittsburgh-type player," said fellow Pirate Al Martin. "He grinds it out every day. We always knew he could hit. We didn't know he was a team player and an all-around gold glove in center field. He's the man here. He's playing well and he's having fun. He keeps me in stitches."

For Giles, it was a dream to make the majors, and even better because his brother made it, too.

"We both wanted to play professional," Brian Giles said, "but we didn't dwell on it all the time."

Although the Pirates did not make a bad trade when they shipped Giles to San Diego (acquiring Jason Bay, plus more), it was a surprise. There was a feeling that when Giles' contract was up he was going to try to return to his home Southern California area.

Giles played his last seven seasons in the big leagues with the Padres, twice hitting .300 and once leading the NL in RBIs. But he never made another All-Star game after leaving Pittsburgh.

> ***All the jokes end when I walk out on that mound.***
>
> – Kent Tekulve

39
KENT TEKULVE

Kent Tekulve is the Pirates' all-time leader with 158 saves and he pitched in 722 games for Pittsburgh, the second-most in team history behind Roy Face. Tekulve also posted a superb overall earned run average with Pittsburgh—2.68.

Born in 1947 in Cincinnati, Tekulve grew up in Ohio and attended Marietta College. He was signed by the Pirates, but did not reach the majors until he was 27 in 1974. Tekulve, who was built a bit like a crane at 6-foot-4 and 160-to-180 pounds, had a distinctive throwing style. He unleashed his pitches with a submarine-type motion.

It was a long road for Tekulve to the majors, but he stayed around a long time, too, for 16 years, into his 40s. Eleven-plus years of Tekulve's career were spent with the Pirates and his shining moment was the role he played in bringing a World Series title to Pittsburgh in 1979. Tekulve saved three of the Pirates' four victories.

Lifetime, Tekulve finished 94-90 with 184 saves after compiling most of his record with Pittsburgh. Tekulve was also known for his durability. He appeared in 1,050 big-league games and every single one of those showings was in relief. He never started a game. Four times Tekulve led the National League in games pitched, three times with the Pirates and once with the Philadelphia Phillies.

Tekulve had three seasons when he pitched in 90 or more games in a season (two with the Pirates) and a fourth year when he played in 85. Tekulve relieved 94 times in 1979, a year after he relieved in 91 games. Later, with the Philllies he had a third 90-game season.

"I have the kind of arm that doesn't tighten up," Tekulve said. "Maybe that's because there are no muscles in it. I'm somewhere between sidearm and submarine, but the reason I'm effective is not so much where the ball is coming from as that it's coming from a different spot."

The lanky thrower, who resembles actor Donald Sutherland with a fastball, had eight seasons when his earned run average was in the 2.00s and an additional year when he finished with a 1.64 mark.

No one reveled in the 1979 Series championship more than Tekulve, who had waited a long time for such success and also played such a significant role in the Pirates' triumph. That October was Tekulve's showcase and having the chance to show off was a bit of vindication. Throughout his life Tekulve was often teased about being so tall and thin. "Hey, kid, go hide behind a rake!" is one example of the kind of jokes he heard. He just never looked like an athlete.

In high school Tekulve tried just about every angle and avenue to gain weight from drinking milk shakes to protein shakes and signing up for the Charles Atlas deals that used to be advertised in the back of comic books. Nothing worked. Since many people do judge a book by its cover, when Tekulve came into pitch he sometimes took grief.

"All the jokes end when I walk out on that mound," Tekulve said.

When it came to quick-judgment tryout camps nothing worked to Tekulve's advantage. Scouts told him he didn't throw fast enough. Others didn't think he looked like a pitching stud. He ended up getting a minor-league contract from the Pirates and spending seven years in the minors before getting his first call to Pittsburgh.

"Everyone was convinced I couldn't do it, except me," Tekulve said. "I was the only one who thought I could. I just kept doing it until I proved I could."

The responsibility of the relief pitcher who finished games was different when Tekulve pitched than it is today. The closer of the 2000s may pitch an inning. When Tekulve was appearing in all of those games he was sometimes pitching 130 innings in a year and he topped 100 seven times. He also got more decisions, going 10-1 in 1977, and 12-8 in 1982.

The Pirates used Tekulve so frequently he got into more games than position-player backups. He said throwing in games 90 or so times was more than he wanted and he didn't want to keep doing it.

"Ideally, I just want to pitch when I'm needed, when I can help the ball club the most," Tekulve said.

Actually, that comment pretty much defined the modern closer job.

When Tekulve set the National League record for most appearances by a pitcher in 1986 he broke Roy Face's record.

"I think it's a record that says I've been a durable pitcher for a long time and that I've been a pitcher who has been effective enough to be used frequently," he said.

He kept rolling to those 1,050 appearances, currently ranked as the ninth most in Major League history.

Courtesy of the National Baseball Hall of Fame Library

One of the three Alou brothers who played in the same outfield for the San Francisco Giants, **Matty Alou** had his greatest success with the Pirates in the late 1960s and early 1970s winning a National League batting title.

40
MATTY ALOU

Although he had been a big leaguer since 1960 Matty Alou did not turn into a real hitter until 1966 when he joined the Pittsburgh Pirates. Until then he was best known as a member of the trio of Alou brothers who had set a record of sorts by playing in the San Francisco Giants outfield together. Matty was the middle brother, younger than Felipe, and older than Jesus.

He was a so-so player until the Pirates tinkered with his swing and suddenly he became a star. Alou joined the Pirates in 1966 and hit .342, winning the National League batting title. He was a member of the Pirates for just five seasons and successively hit .338, .332, .331 and .297 after his debut. In 1969 he also led the NL in hits with 231.

A lefty swinger and a lefty thrower, Alou grew up in the Dominican Republic and was in the first wave of major leaguers from that baseball-mad country. Primarily an outfielder, Matty Alou stood just 5-foot-9 and weighed 160 pounds. He was not a power hitter, but a great contact hitter over the course of his 15-year big-league career which ended in 1974. Some viewed his stature and called him "The Mouse."

Alou was no power hitter and padded his batting average with the shortest hits a batter can get—bunts. When he won the batting crown Alou counted 23 bunt hits among his 183 safeties.

"I always bunt good," he said.

When Matty won the title he edged out brother Felipe, who finished second in the race at .327. That was a first. Other Pirates, Paul and Lloyd Waner, came close to notching the feat first, but finished 1-3.

Although Alou did hit .310 in 81 games for the Giants in 1961, in 1965, the season before the Pirates acquired him he hit just .231 for San Francisco. Pirates manager Harry Walker was a strong influence in getting Alou's hitting stroke straightened out. He urged him to choke up on the bat handle a little bit and not pull everything. That simple advice produced a transformation so drastic that teammate Bill Virdon thought he was looking at two different hitters, not a before and after same man.

"I can't believe he's the same batter I saw for the last time in 1965," the Pirates center fielder said. "He's made a believer out of me."

Some Pittsburgh sportswriters who had witnessed the same change took to calling Alou's bat a "magic wand." It might as well have been. Alou adapted so well that he was getting base hits to all fields with startling regularity.

"We just scatter nine men and pray," said Atlanta Braves manager Luman Harris of his team's defensive strategy against Alou.

The funny part was that Alou's form at the plate was ugly, so unusual that Ted Williams, that scientific genius of batting who was managing the Washington Senators in an exhibition game against the Pirates was pretty much aghast.

"He violates every hitting principle I ever taught," Williams said.

Oh yes, Alou was wielding a 40-ounce bat to do his damage, the kind of weapon a much larger man used decades earlier, but which seemingly had been retired along with the silent movies.

"Matty swings a bat so heavy I'm afraid to pick it up," said Pirate second baseman Bill Mazeroski.

All Alou did was smack singles and doubles with amazing consistency. In 1969 he led the National League with 41 doubles. Home runs, though, were definitely an endangered species in his life. Some seasons Alou hit exactly zero four-baggers. During his time with Pittsburgh the most RBIs Alou collected was 52. He was a table-setter, not a table clearer.

Alou was accumulating so many hits that season when he totaled 231 that it generated interest in the press about whether he might break Paul Waner's team record of 237 that had been around since 1927.

"Those records," Alou said, "I don't know about them. I just swing the bat and then once or twice a week somebody asks me about records. I try not to think about them."

Alou was dismissed as a fluke after his first huge hitting season in Pittsburgh, but when he continued to record high averages opponents doffed their caps to him. Alou admitted that not even he believed that Walker's suggestions would make such a difference—110 points in one year—in his hitting.

"I listened to Harry when I first got to camp," Alou said. "I figured what did I have to lose? When you hit only .231 you had better listen to someone."

Although the Pirates chose to trade Alou in 1971, he had more hitting in him, recording two more .300 seasons and two more .290s years before retiring with a .305 average.

Courtesy of the National Baseball Hall of Fame Library

Possessor of an intimidating fastball, southpaw **Bob Veale** was a strikeout king in the late 1960s and early 1970s and seven times won at least 10 games for the Pirates in a season.

41
BOB VEALE

The big southpaw could make batters quake in their cleats. Bob Veale stood 6-foot-6 and weighed a good 230 pounds and standing on the mound he looked like a giant to the hitters inhabiting the batter's box. Veale possessed a wicked fast fastball and even more frightening for the hitters, he did not have pinpoint control. He led the National League in walks and was right up there in strikeouts every year.

Born in Alabama in 1935, Veale attended St. Benedict's College in Kansas before breaking into the majors with the Pirates in 1962. He was already 26. He spent five years in the minors getting to the big-league roster. Veale stuck with Pittsburgh until 1972 and except for a handful or so of games pitched for the Boston Red Sox spent his entire Major League career hurling for the Pirates.

Veale's lifetime record was 120-95 and all but 4-4 of it came while wearing a Pittsburgh uniform. His lifetime earned run average was a very good 3.07. The towering southpaw (who happened to be a switch-hitter) was a two-time All-Star for the Pirates, gaining NL recognition in 1965 and 1966.

In 1964, Veale struck out 250 men to lead the league in Ks. Three other times Veale fanned more than 200 batters, putting up seasonal totals of 276, 229 and 213. It is quite possible that the fact Veale wore oversized looking glasses also made batters a bit nervous.

Walks aside, Veale balanced the scales with those strikeouts and that led to victory totals of 18, 17, 16, and 16 for Pittsburgh.

Initially, with Veale's blazing fastball, Pirates brass thought he would be a weapon out of the bullpen, a short-inning man who could come in to intimidate and quell rallies. That experiment didn't last long, especially when Veale got the chance to start and mowed down opponents, in one case posting a 16-strikeout effort against the Cincinnati Reds in a game where he was still pitching in the 13th inning. Another time Veale struck out 16 against the Phillies as part of a five-hit shutout. It was obvious that Veale could be a longer-lasting weapon than just popping into games for a late-inning cameo. The 16 Ks in a game was a team record.

One of the more amazing aspects of the Phillies game was that rain interruptions caused the game to go almost four-and-a-half hours. Veale stuck with it throughout. The game ran past midnight and while Veale confessed he was a bit tired (even if catcher Jim Pagliaroni kept telling him he wasn't) he was aware of the length.

"This is the first time I've ever pitched two days running," he said.

Veale could remember days when he was throwing just as fast, but the results weren't the same.

"I always had a strikeout pitch, or strikeout pitches, but had trouble controlling them," Veale said. Referring to a minor-league game he said, "I once struck out 22 Buffalo batters for Columbus, but I left with the score 5-5."

Basically, Veale harnessed his talent as he learned to pitch instead of merely throw and one rather interested and sharp observer of that change was the Giants' Willie Mays.

"That may sound funny, but when he threw hard he didn't know where the ball was going," Mays said. "Since he let up a little on his fastball, he throws strikes."

Veale was a good all-around athlete. He liked to take his cuts in the batter's box and he was a college track man with about 9.8-second speed in the 100-yard dash. He also played basketball. Veale said he had feelers from the American Basketball League about going pro in that sport in the early 1960s. But on the whole he preferred to throw.

One of the things Veale developed by perhaps taking some of the oomph off of his throws was the ability to stay fast deeper into games. Phillies manager Gene Mauch said, "It was the longest fire I've ever seen." He meant that Veale was throwing just as fast at the end of the game as at the beginning.

Veale did admit that he sometimes drew motivation if someone or something made him a little bit mad leading up to, or in a game. Referring to one contest against the Reds, in which he pitched a shutout, he said he threw "angry ball. I get provoked at myself when I do things wrong. And when I get upset, I throw harder."

Veale definitely had numerous special moments for the Pirates and when he put all of his attributes together they occurred more frequently.

"I've come to the conclusion that rhythm and deception are the main ingredients in pitching," Veale said. "The secret is coordinating rhythm and deception and putting the ball where you want to."

> ***To be up there with all those names, not just the Pirates, but the names (of other batting champs), it feels good.***
>
> – Freddy Sanchez

42
FREDDY SANCHEZ

His candle did not give off a bright light for too long in Pittsburgh, but at his best Freddy Sanchez was a star second baseman for the Pirates who hit as well as anybody in the National League.

Born in Hollywood, California in 1977, Sanchez attended Dallas Baptist and Oklahoma City University before being drafted by the Boston Red Sox. The 6-foot, 200-pound infielder came to the Pirates in a five-player deal prior to the 2004 season.

Less than two years later Sanchez tore up the NL in a shocking performance. Sanchez won the 2006 National League batting crown with a .344 average. He also stroked 200 hits, led the league with 53 doubles, scored 85 runs and collected 85 runs batted in. Sanchez's season came under the heading of overnight sensation since he began the season as a utility infielder on Pittsburgh's depth chart.

In four full seasons and parts of two others, Sanchez was a three-time All-Star for the Pirates and twice hit .300 or better.

During that breakthrough season Sanchez did not even earn a place in the starting lineup until May. By the end of it not only did every fan know his name he was voted the winner of the Roberto Clemente Award for following the standards of excellence personified by the Pirate great.

Sanchez was fairly surprised at the lofty status he had acquired in the space of just a few months.

"To be up there with all those names, not just the Pirates, but the names (of other batting champs), it feels good," Sanchez said. "Who would have thought at the beginning of the year I'd be in this situation?"

Never mind the beginning of the year, no one really expected that Sanchez would win a batting championship regardless of how long he played.

At the very end of the season, when it was apparent that Sanchez had won the batting title, members of the Pirates stood and gave him an ovation. At the time it was Pittsburgh's first batting title victor in 23 years, or since Bill Madlock captured a crown.

"It's just been a great day for him," said Pirates shortstop Jack Wilson, including the fact that Sanchez wound up the campaign with two hits to reach that 200 milestone. "The last couple of months watching him do what he does, I enjoyed watching him more than the year I had my 200 hits. He's the epitome of consistency for a major-league hitter."

Wilson and Sanchez were old friends. They played together on a California summer league squad years earlier.

Such compliments from seen-it-all teammates are hard to come by, but that was the type of splash Sanchez made over those summer months in 2006. Sanchez was in a tight race with Miguel Cabrera, then representing the Florida Marlins and just beginning his extraordinary career. The Pirates were well down in the standings and so fans focused their rooting attention on Sanchez's quest. Many in the stands held up signs reading "Go Freddy Go."

Sanchez admitted to being a little bit tense, but when he cracked a single in the first inning he became far more relaxed.

"That first hit took a load off," Sanchez said. "There was a lot of relief."

Sanchez was thought of more as a glove man than as a big-time swinger, so the Pirates reaped the results as a pleasant enough surprise, too. Pittsburgh was in one of its long-term rebuilding phases, hoping young players like Sanchez represented a brighter future.

"Freddy Sanchez really embodies what we as an organization want this franchise to be," said manager Jim Tracy. "He has all the attributes of a winning player, personality, hard work and a very competitive nature. He's a tremendous overachiever, a very talented overachiever. He can really hit."

Cabrera went oh-for-two in his first at-bats on the final day of the season and then left the game because Sanchez was uncatchable. Sanchez added one more hit.

"It really hasn't sunk in yet," Sanchez said after the game. "I'll go home and relax for a couple of days and have a chance to think back on it. And I'll be like, 'Wow! This is something special.'"

It was indeed the high point of Sanchez's career, not only with the Pirates. The next year Sanchez batted .304 and then he dipped to .271. He was hitting .296 111 games into the 2009 season, a year when he became the first Pirate in 19 years to have a six-hit game, when the Pirates traded him to the San Francisco Giants for a minor-league player named Tim Alderson.

Sanchez had rejected a long-term offer from the Pirates, but was hopeful of more negotiation. Instead he was traded and ended his career with the Giants at 33 because of shoulder and back surgeries.

> ***Nobody gives you anything in this game. You have to earn it.***
>
> – Don Hoak

43
DON HOAK

His numbers weren't as impressive as many great Pirates of the past, but Don Hoak was a player who made as much impact with his attitude and his mouth as his bat and glove, especially in 1960 when he was the third baseman for the 1960 World Series champions.

Hoak was born in 1928 in Roulette, Pennsylvania, about 180 miles from Pittsburgh, but it was the Brooklyn Dodgers that offered him a path to the majors. Hoak was 6-foot-1 and weighed 175 pounds. He was a former Marine, a hard-nosed player who did not break into the big leagues until 1954 when he was 26.

Of the 11 years Hoak spent in the majors only four of them were with the Pirates, but three of them were special. In those four seasons Hoak batted .294, .282, .298 and .241.

In 1960, when Hoak was the runner-up as National League Most Valuable Player to teammate Dick Groat, he hit 16 home runs, drove in 79 runs, scored 97, and hit .282. He was the fiery on-field leader for the pennant winners, the heart and soul of a top-notch team that is one of the most fondly remembered in Pirates history.

Hoak was nicknamed "Tiger" and that's because he brought a killer instinct to the game. He played in 380 consecutive games, and was a take-charge player who spoke up in the dugout and on the field. When it came to body language Hoak was proud, defiant, and confident, challenging pitchers to get him out.

Besides his stint in the Marines, Hoak earned some stripes for toughness while dabbling in a career as a boxer. He won 27 of 39 fights.

"I fought as a welterweight and a middleweight, but soon found this wasn't the life for me," Hoak said. "I averaged about $25 a fight and broke my nose so often I gave it up for baseball."

He never pretended that he was the most purely talented player on the block, but Hoak displayed a feistiness that showed everyone how determined he was to win. Winning was what turned him on and losing was what bugged him.

"I have to play hard to make up for my limited skills," Hoak said. "Nobody gives you anything in this game. You have to earn it."

While it is not well-remembered, Hoak actually appeared in the 1955 World Series for the Dodgers—and hit .333. He also was a regular in winter ball and one year in Cuba Hoak was at the plate when the action paused because the revolutionary leader and his followers came to the ball park. The individual grabbed a glove, strode to the mound and threw to Hoak. That was Fidel Castro, who loved baseball, was proud of his talent, but was more interested in fomenting political change.

When Hoak was traded from the Cincinnati Reds to the Pirates he was determined to make big changes in Pittsburgh. Along with Harvey Haddix and Smoky Burgess, the deal brought Hoak and bought a pennant. He played very well, but what Hoak delivered was a style of leadership.

"Don is the straw boss of the team," Groat said of Hoak in 1960. "The way he gets on the rest of us should peel the skin off our backs, but when you're trying to win a pennant you need somebody whose tongue can lash you like a whip. Hoak is the one and we all respect him for his desire."

Hoak was both the king of pep talks and the constant critic and motivator. He worked over anyone whom he thought was flagging because he recognized as the 1960 schedule turned for home the Pirates had a chance to claim their first pennant since 1927.

"We're going to win," he said. "We got the best team. We make the fewest mistakes. There are 25 guys on this club with the best spirit I've ever seen. We don't need power in our ballpark (spacious Forbes Field). We're able to get runs without it. We can move runners along. Anybody makes a mistake against us gets his brains knocked out."

He was right that year, but not in 1961 when he thought Pittsburgh could defend. But Hoak played with fire. He had an ankle injury in spring training and rested it, but said if it was opening day he would "just spit on the ankle and play."

After Hoak retired, he was a Pirates broadcaster for two years, worked as a Phillies coach, and was a manager in the Pirates minor-league system hoping to one day take over the big club. However, he died of a heart attack prematurely at only 41 in 1969.

Hoak's old teammates were shocked because they viewed him as indestructible.

"Are you sure it was Don?" said Donn Clendenon. "Oh, my God."

"***I decided to relax when I pitched and I never was so amazed.***"

– Steve Blass

44
STEVE BLASS

As a rookie in 1964 Steve Blass went 5-8. He made it back to the big club in 1966 and remained with Pittsburgh for all 10 of his Major League seasons, going 103-76 with a 3.63 earned run average.

At his best the righty born in Connecticut in 1942 was better than most. At his worst, when things went haywire in one of the most publicized cases of a player making a swift, virtually inexplicable descent to the bottom, fans and teammates felt sorry for him.

Blass got off to a good start, winning his debut game 4-2 over the Los Angeles Dodgers, and showing he had the stuff of a big leaguer.

"I had a little trouble getting to sleep Sunday night knowing I was to pitch the next evening," Blass said, "and I was nervous before the game, too, but it all turned out well."

It took a little bit of time for Blass to find his rhythm, but wisdom imparted by pitching coach Clyde King helped him adapt to the majors. King was constantly after Blass to relax.

"I seemed so tense every time I pitched I just threw blindly," Blass said.

It is one thing for someone to tell a player to relax and quite another for a player to make it happen, to conquer whatever distractions might cloud his mind.

"I decided to relax when I pitched and I never was so amazed," Blass said of a key game. "My ball did tricks and I could put the ball just about any place I wanted to."

In 1968 Blass finished 18-6 with a 2.12 earned run average. In 1971, when the Pirates won the World Series, Blass finished 15-8 with a 2.85 ERA.

Blass was a big reason why Pittsburgh won the Series over the Baltimore Orioles. Blass started two games and won both, pitching two complete games. His Series ERA was 1.00. They definitely made room on the float for Blass in the celebratory parade.

For Blass, 1971 was the most memorable of his career. That was also the season when he gave wearing glasses a try so that he could see home plate 60 feet, 6 inches away from the mound. There were suggestions that if Blass saw a sharper view of reality he might be a better pitcher. Only that wasn't the case. The funny thing was that Blass' eyesight wasn't even good enough for him to pick up the normal one finger, two fingers hand signs for calling pitches from catcher Manny Sanguillen.

"The fingers don't mean nothing," said Sanguillen, who realized he had a special case to deal with. "I give him signs other ways. I touch my leg here, or here, or I touch this shoulder, or this one."

Blass just said no to glasses after trying them in batting practice. He then proclaimed they were OK for watching TV or going to the movies, but not for wearing in games.

Blass' last great season was 1972. He compiled an 18-9 record with a 2.49 earned run average. He was still at the top of his game and figured to have several more good seasons, especially because of his late start in the majors. Blass only 32, a pitcher in his prime, was surely headed for better seasons. But those better seasons never came.

Suddenly, inexplicably, Blass lost his control. He wound up the same way. He threw the same, but he couldn't throw the ball over the plate. There was no obvious way to understand what was going wrong. There was no major injury. Nothing showed up when his arm was X-rayed. Somehow between his excellent 1972 season and the 1973 season Blass completely lost the ability to throw pitches in the strike zone.

The astonishing development very much seemed like the onset of an incurable disease. Overnight Blass' career was ruined and what happened to him became known as "Steve Blass Disease." Only 31—when he should have been in his prime—Blass went 3-9 with a 9.85 earned run average in 1973, pitched just one game in 1974, and was out of the sport.

"I can't blame anybody but myself," Blass said. "And yet it's hard to blame myself when there seems to be no valid reason for what happened."

Later, Blass, whose sudden demise remains a mystery, became a long-term and very popular Pirates broadcast commentator, a role he remains in after 30 years. In 2009, while playing in the annual Pirates alumni golf tournament Blass, then 67, made two holes-in-one in the same round, a feat rated as 67 million to 1 by Golf Digest.

"I can finally make some kind of ball go where I want it to," Blass joked. "Maybe it's a sign from above that I should start pitching again."

> ***Life is a mystery to be lived, not a problem to be solved.***
>
> – John Candelaria

45
JOHN CANDELARIA

The Candy Man made Pittsburgh Pirates history in August of 1976 when he pitched a no-hit, 2-0 victory over the Los Angeles Dodgers. The 6-foot-7 left-hander was hardly touched by the opposing batters, a running catch by outfielder David Parker on a sinking shot was the only thing close to a safety. Only three runners reached base, though L.A. did jam the bases in the third inning.

"I feel fantastic," said Candelaria, who was 23 at the time. "Just great. I was very nervous in the last inning. I was just trying to keep the ball down, trying to get them one at a time. It's just tremendous."

The Brooklyn-raised Candelaria was born in 1953 and drafted by the Pirates in 1972. He made his big-league debut in 1975 and his signature Major League season was the 1977 campaign when he finished 20-5 with a National League-leading earned run average of 2.34.

Still, Candelaria could recount an even more exciting moment than hurling a no-hitter.

"My biggest thrill was when I won my first big-league game before 53,000 people, including my mother, at Shea Stadium," Candelaria said. He finished 8-6 as a rookie, with an impressive 2.76 earned run average.

Candelaria spent the first 10-plus years of his 19-year big-league career with the Pirates and eight times won at least 10 games in a season for Pittsburgh.

Bushy-haired and lean at 220 pounds, Candelaria's biggest problems during his career revolved around recurring injuries which flared up when he was still a very young man. Even after his no-hitter Candelaria said he experienced back pain after every game he threw.

"I always hurt more the day after I pitch," he said. "It would be hurting even if I had been knocked out in the first inning or if I pitched five or six innings."

Candelaria immediately became popular in Pittsburgh, with the fans, and management. Manager Chuck Tanner said his man's future was bright.

"He's young and he pitches like a man much older," Tanner said. "He can win when he doesn't have his best stuff. That's the sign of an outstanding pitcher." Candelaria was "the best left-hander in the league. I wouldn't trade Candy for (Steve) Carlton. Our man is younger and he's going to get better and better."

That prognosis did not prove to be accurate, however. Carlton became a Hall of Famer and Candelaria remained a solid pitcher who had to overcome difficulties, although he did win 177 games in his career. Never mind the back aches, more critically for a pitcher Candelaria ran into frequent arm problems that trimmed the edge off his fastball. He also had personal problems, going through a divorce.

After showing his early promise Candelaria's career ran off the rails and he struggled almost non-stop from 1978 to 1983 when he proclaimed himself injury free.

"I think I'm picking up the speed again on my fastball," he said. "Maybe I won't be the power pitcher that I was, but I'm still a fastball pitcher. It's no secret what I'm going to throw when I'm in trouble. I'm sure not going to throw my second-best pitch when I'm behind."

After the brilliant 20-5 campaign, for which he was selected to his only All-Star team, Candelaria's totals went like this: 12-11, 14-9, 11-14, 2-2, and 12-7. The 14-9 season was accompanied by a 3.22 earned run average and contributed to the Pirates winning the World Series in 1979. He won a game in the Series over the Baltimore Orioles. And all did seem right with the world again in '83 when he finished 15-8.

However, when Candelaria's arm gave him aggravation he was sometimes assigned to the bullpen to sort things out, no longer a key member of the Pirates rotation. It was double frustration for him. Away from the mound Candelaria seemed to be equal parts charm, childish, and colorful. He was once arrested for roller skating on a highway and once dispensed $238 worth of meal money one dollar at a time from the team bus on the way to Wrigley Field.

"Life is a mystery to be lived, not a problem to be solved," he said.

That changed, though, when his toddler son fell into a swimming pool, fell into a long-term coma, and then died. That was a problem that could not be solved and the good-natured Candelaria's attitude was altered by the tragedy, as he was haunted by his loss.

In 1985 the Pirates traded Candelaria to the California Angels. Over the next several years he bounced from team to team, often pitching in relief. In 1993 he returned to Pittsburgh for a last fling, but after going 0-3 with an 8.24 ERA he was cut and retired at 39.

"It's been a wild trip," Candelaria said.

> ***Most of my decision was made on how this organization came to me when I was a nobody and gave me the opportunity to have the life I have today.***
>
> – Al Martin

46
AL MARTIN

Outfielder Al Martin broke into the majors with the Pirates in 1992 at 24 with the assignment of replacing Barry Bonds in left field. It was a daunting task, but Martin, while not an All-Star, did a very solid job for the Pirates. He spent eight of his 11 Major League seasons in Pittsburgh.

Although it was portrayed that way by sportswriters, Martin kept his perspective when he said, "I'm not replacing Barry Bonds. I am merely playing the same position that Barry played in Pittsburgh."

Born in West Covina, California in 1967, Martin was a 6-foot-2, 220-pound player who could hit for power, but generally took his opportunities where he found them. He hit some homers, drove in some runs, and hit for a very respectable average.

A typically fine Martin season was produced in 1993, his first full season in the majors. Martin hit 18 home runs, drove in 64 runs, scored 85 runs, and stole 16 bases, all while batting .281. The all-around nature of Martin's game is what made him such a valuable contributor.

Generally very consistent, Martin's best single-season total for the Pirates in the key hitting categories were 101 runs scored, 72 runs batted in, 24 home runs, and a .300 average.

Martin was originally drafted by the Atlanta Braves, but never played in the majors for them before joining the Pirates. He viewed the team switch as good a good thing.

"As soon as I came over here last year," Martin said in his second season in Pittsburgh, "I knew I had a chance. It's different when you're in an organization knowing that no matter what you do, you won't even make the team. Here, I had the opportunity. I just had to take advantage of it, and be the best player I can be."

The Pirates were in transition when Martin came to Pittsburgh and he endured some difficult seasons with the club, though as personnel changed he became an elder statesman and leader on the field. He was only 29, yet was a Pirate with longevity because of tremendous turnover.

"I've been a leader on this team for a while," Martin said. "Not the leader, but one of the leaders, and that's not going to change. But as far as being a veteran, that's a different story because you usually have a guy who has 10 or 12 years and you can go talk to."

The Pirates had just come off some good years and were rebuilding, seemingly from scratch, when Martin was thrown into the mix. They didn't know they were in for a long, long losing streak.

"I hate losing," Martin said. "But the good thing about baseball is you can lose and have a bad game, and in less than 24 hours you can lace them up and play again. It's going to take some time for us to grow."

Almost unimaginably, the Pirates were embarking on a journey that resulted in two decades straight of losing seasons.

Martin loyally stuck with the Pirates when he didn't have to sign new contracts.

"Most of my decision was made on how this organization came to me when I was a nobody and gave me the opportunity to have the life I have today," Martin said five years into his Pirates tenure.

Later in his career, after Martin was no longer a Pirate, discrepancies in his official biography tarnished his image a bit. Claims that he had played college football at Southern California and that he had been named to a National League All-Star team, but didn't play because of injury, were incorrect.

47
BILL VIRDON

Outfielder Bill Virdon was a rookie of the year with the St. Louis Cardinals, but he was part of the glue that held together the Pirates during their 1960 World Series run, playing a brilliant center field. A savvy player who was later a successful manager, Virdon did not always carry a big stick, but he always seemed to be around the action.

Virdon was born in Michigan in 1931, but attended high school in Missouri. He stood 6 feet tall and weighed 175 pounds and was very quick, always getting a good jump on the ball in the field. The New York Yankees, one of the teams Virdon would later manage, signed him as a free agent in 1950. It was not easy for Virdon to get noticed because his high school had no baseball team.

"I played anything that they played," Virdon said. "I played football, basketball, ran track. I played in one high school baseball game. My senior year the coach decided he was going to try and get baseball started. We ended up playing one game against a nearby school."

He did end up playing summer ball at the Ban Johnson League level and that's where he was signed. Virdon got as close as spring training to making the Yankees, but went 0-for-19 and was traded to the Cardinals. He considered that to be a good break because the Yankees had a glut of outfielders. It was more surprising when he was traded to Pittsburgh for Bobby Del Greco and David Littlefield in 1956.

As a big leaguer Virdon played 12 seasons and 10 of them were for the Pirates. A .267 lifetime hitter, Virdon's best season at-bat was .334 in 1956. He generally hit about eight home runs a year and drove in about 50 runs.

In one game in 1958 Virdon threw out two runners at the plate in a single inning. In 1962 Virdon won a Gold Glove and he also led the National League with 10 triples. No matter what Virdon did at the plate he was admired for what he accomplished in the field where he combined good range, a good arm and good judgment to make great plays.

"As far as I'm concerned, Virdon is the best in the field," said Pirate reliever Roy Face. "He's as good as Willie Mays and I can't make it stronger than that. Virdon is a comfort to the pitchers because he does his job so well. The best compliment I can pay him is when a ball is hit in his direction with two outs I automatically start walking off the mound."

In the late 1950s and early 1960s Virdon was always among the league leaders in putouts and assists for outfielders. He pursued every ball with a vengeance.

"We pitchers make him chase our mistakes, but he always does the job," said Pirate starter Harvey Haddix. "Virdon is as good as any of them."

Whether it was additional wear and tear from roaming the wide open spaces of Forbes Field, or something else, Virdon felt he was coming to the end of the line as a starter at a fairly young age.

"I'll be 34 in June," he said in 1965, "and no sense kidding myself, I can't last too long as a day-to-day player. I could feel myself slipping a little last season, and when you get older every step is a bit longer."

Virdon knew all along he wanted to become a manager and he did, leading the Pirates, New York Yankees, Houston Astros and Montreal Expos. Virdon won three manager-of-the-year awards.

48
DICK STUART

The nickname bestowed upon Dick Stuart said it all about the indifferent quality of his fielding at first base: Dr. Strangeglove. But Stuart lived to hit and had most of his fun in baseball swinging for the fences. He was renowned for his ability to swing and miss as well, but Stuart did blast many prodigious home runs.

Sometimes it seemed as if it was a toss-up whether Stuart actually got more of a kick out of belting home runs or talking about home runs. He developed that habit after smashing 66 dingers in the Western League playing for Lincoln, Nebraska in 1956.

Born in San Francisco in 1932, Stuart was a powerfully built 6-foot-4 and 220 pounds. Between getting out of the minors, performing military service, and losing his swing at a fairly early age, Stuart spent just 10 years in the majors, five with the Pirates. He also had some notable success with the Boston Red Sox.

As a rookie in 1958 Stuart made a splash when he cracked his first big-league home run and followed it up with something bigger.

"My first big-league home run Thursday and a day later my first grand slam!" Stuart said. "I'll always remember Wrigley Field in Chicago and the Cubs."

At his best, Stuart did live up to the hype that swirled around him (much of it self-created after that huge minor-league homer campaign). In 1960, when the Pirates won the World Series, Stuart hit 23 home runs and drove in 83 runs. In 1961 Stuart blasted 35 homers, drove in 117 runs, and batted .301. Hitting for a high average was an aberration—Stuart's lifetime average was .264.

The Pirates won that World Series on second baseman Bill Mazeroski's memorable walk-off home run. Stuart was waiting for his turn at bat in the on-deck circle and hoping for a chance to end the game against the Yankees in the same way.

"I was kneeling in the on-deck circle," Stuart said, "thinking I was going to be the hero. All of a sudden, I was out on the field jumping around."

Stuart's fielding was so bad that he was often ridiculed for not handling that aspect of the game. His career came along too early, or else he would have been the perfect designated hitter. As a player whose only job was to hit, Stuart would have fit right in.

"Dick's biggest problem was his lack of concentration," said teammate Dick Groat. "Thinking about hitting instead of playing defense. It wasn't that his hands were so bad. Dick just wanted to hit the ball. He didn't want to be catching it or fighting ground balls. To Dick, fielding was a necessary evil."

Stuart did make magic with his bat, though. During a home game against the Cubs in 1959, Stuart became the first player to hit a ball over the center field wall. At that point the park was 50 years old. The ball traveled over the 457-foot mark and Chicago outfielder George Altman estimated that it cleared the fence by 25 or 30 feet.

"I knew I hit it good when I connected," Stuart said.

In one game during the 1960 season Stuart smacked three home runs and drove in seven runs against the San Francisco Giants.

"I wanted a fourth home run badly," said Stuart afterwards of his hopes of tying the big-league record, "but didn't think Bud Byerly would throw me a strike. Then I thought to myself maybe he'll try to be cute and throw one, figuring I'm not looking for it."

Stuart grounded out to third.

49
DOCK ELLIS

Right-handed pitcher Dock Ellis was born in California in 1945 and was drafted by the Pirates in 1964. He made his Major League debut with Pittsburgh in 1968 when he went 6-5 with a 2.50 earned run average, and spent eight-plus of his 12 years in the majors with the Pirates.

Ellis was 6-foot-3 and weighed 205 pounds and had several very good seasons for the Pirates. In 1972 he was at his best, going 19-9 and being named an All-Star for the only time in his career. Ellis was 15-7 in 1972 and 17-8 in 1976.

In later years, the sometimes funky, often outrageous Ellis, became better known for confessing that he pitched a no-hitter while under the influence of LSD. In 1984 Ellis revealed that he had taken LSD before pitching the special game for the Pirates in 1970 against the San Diego Padres.

"I can only remember bits and pieces of the game," said Ellis, who was an admitted drug addict who got clean and worked as a drug counselor. "I was psyched. I had a feeling of euphoria. I was zeroed in on the glove, but I didn't hit the glove too much. I remember hitting a couple of batters and the bases were loaded two or three times."

Ellis made it clear that he wanted to have fun off the field and although he had fallen into pitching as a profession it had not always been his life's dream. That was because he ran with a rough crowd in Watts, got arrested sometimes, and played basketball and ran track at Gardena High when he was playing sports. He did find baseball in a semi-pro league.

Courtesy of the National Baseball Hall of Fame Library

Dock Ellis was one of the funkiest players to represent the Pirates. He claimed that he pitched a no-hitter while tripping on LSD.

"All I knew about pitching then was throwing fastballs," Ellis said. "I had to find out the hard way that when it's 3-and-2 on the hitter, you throw breaking stuff outside. Man, I hardly knew what a curve and a slider were back then."

Ellis' father died when he was 18 and his mother always told Ellis he was just like him except that his father saved money and he spent his money. Later, Ellis said. "Man, I want to live, really enjoy life. Right now." He came to the ballpark wearing suits or sometimes brightly colored outfits, including his shoes. Ellis talked non-stop, so much, indeed, that one sportswriter referred to his mouth as "heavily muscled from constant use." During the 1973 season Ellis experimented with hair curlers in the clubhouse seeking a way to keep his hairdo straight.

Ellis and others realized he had a learning curve, but that he had the goods to become one of the best pitchers in the National League.

"I believe that Ellis has better all-around stuff than Bob Gibson," said former Pirate star Vern Law. "He still has to learn how to use it in order to be a big winner."

Experience helped tutor Ellis and he became a better pitcher as he learned the trade. He employed more change-ups and said, "I'm using it more. That gives them another pitch to think about."

Ellis was pitching very well in 1973, sitting on a 12-9 record with a 3.05 earned run average when he suffered a broken hand from a line drive ending his year.

Pittsburgh won the 1971 World Series with Ellis on the team and he four times pitched for the Pirates in the National League Championship Series, 1970, 1971, 1972, and 1975. Ellis lost his only start in the Series against the Baltimore Orioles.

Ellis retired from baseball in 1980 and died from a liver ailment in 2008 at 63.

“*Being a big-league ball player means something to all of us. I like signing for the good people—and there are plenty of good people everywhere.*”

– Richie Hebner

50
RICHIE HEBNER

When he was young growing up in Norwood, Massachusetts it seemed more likely that Richie Hebner would end up skating for the Boston Bruins, but the Pirates drafted him in 1966 and by the time he was 20 in 1968 he had appeared in his first Major League game.

Hebner was 6-foot-1 and 185 pounds and for most of his 18-year career the lefty swinger was a third baseman, though he played first later on. Hebner spent 10 years with the Pirates, broken into two stints, the first one of eight years.

Ranked as one of the best high school hockey players in the country, it turned out that when it came to swinging good wood Hebner was better wielding a baseball bat than a hockey stick. A solid hitter, a solid fielder, and a holler guy, Hebner hit a high of 25 homers for Pittsburgh, with a high of 74 runs batted in. He batted .300 twice.

Hebner was a regular on the Pirates' 1971 World Series championship team and batted .333 in the Series against Baltimore. In all, Hebner played in five National League Championship Series for Pittsburgh.

From his mid-teens on Hebner held a part-time job as a grave digger and he kept up the work even after going into professional baseball. Grave digger being a non-traditional off-season job in the minds of many, Hebner caught a lot of heckling grief.

"I get a lot of kidding from the other players about it," Hebner said. "They call me 'Digger' and 'Shoveler" and things like that. But what the heck, I like to work outside in the fresh air."

At one point during Hebner's career the Pirates got the notion that he should become a base stealer.

"If Richie gets a better jump from first he could steal more bases," said Pirates manager Danny Murtaugh.

It was all wishful thinking. Hebner trod heavily and he stole just 38 bases in his entire career.

Hebner was a friendly player and that played well with Pirates fans, especially when they caught up to him and begged for autographs. Hebner was a champion signer who spent considerable time trying to make the people happy. He also talked to the ground crews around the majors and the ushers at Forbes Field.

Once when Hebner was just 21 an official in the commissioner's office stumbled upon him signing his name for about 30 minutes and later thanked him for interacting with the fans.

"Congratulate me…the man congratulated me…for what?" Heber said. The signings were just a regular part of his day. "Being a big-league ball player means something to all of us. I like signing for the good people—and there are plenty of good people everywhere."

Early in his career Hebner was seen chewing tobacco and someone asked him why. He said, "Maybe it helps my looks."

Hebner didn't seem to need any help on that front since he was single and was considered an eligible bachelor-about-town, even if he didn't encourage the image and said it wasn't really true. Hebner spent much of his free time visiting children in hospitals and the area's school for the blind, and he was a good enough Catholic to keep track of when Mass started.

"God gave me a gifted ability," Hebner said. "As a result, I've met a lot of nice people. But I don't think of myself as a superstar. I try to keep a level head. I try to keep out of the limelight."

After Hebner retired from playing he embarked on a second baseball career as a Major League coach and minor-league manager.

Sources

Associated Press
Baseball Magazine
Brooklyn Eagle
Chicago Tribune
Deadball Stars of the National League / Society for American Baseball Research
ESPN.com
MLB.com
National League Service Bureau
Newspaper Enterprise Association
New York Daily News
New York Journal-American
New York Post
Pittsburgh Pirates Media Guide
Pittsburgh Post-Gazette
Pittsburgh Press
Pittsburgh Sun-Telegraph
San Francisco Examiner
Sarasota Herald-Tribune
Saturday Evening Post
Smithsonian Magazine
Sport Magazine
Sports Collectors Digest
St. Louis Post-Dispatch
The Oklahoman
The Sporting News
Tulsa World
United Press

ABOUT THE AUTHOR

Lew Freedman is a veteran sportswriter who is the author of more than 70 books, many on baseball, and has been an avid researcher of baseball history. He has also worked as a sportswriter for the Chicago Tribune, Philadelphia Inquirer, and Anchorage Daily News. He thinks Honus Wagner and Roberto Clemente would make anyone's dream team.